HOMILIES FOR WEDDINGS AND FUNERALS

Joseph Pollard

Homilies for Weddings and Funerals

the columba press

First published in 2004 by
the columba press
55A Spruce Avenue, Stillorgan Industrial Park,
Blackrock, Co Dublin

Cover by Bill Bolger
Origination by The Columba Press
Printed in Ireland by ColourBooks Ltd, Dublin

ISBN 1 85607 448 X

Acknowledgements

Scripture quotations are from the New Revised Standard Version, copyright © 1989, by the Division of Christian Education of the National Council of the Churches of Christ in the United States of America. Used by permission.

Table of Contents

Introduction

Liturgy is celebrated. At root, this simply means that liturgy is conducted with appropriate ritual. However, celebration usually includes the elements of joy and festival. The manner in which these are expressed in ritual differs from wedding to funeral.

The wedding ritual and homily celebrate the special love of the couple about to be married, the joy of their wedding day, and the promise of their future. The funeral liturgy and homily are celebratory in the sense that they gather the community, focus its grief, comfort the bereaved, and celebrate the hope of glory for them in their loss of a loved one.

Weddings and funerals are challenging occasions because they are emotionally charged times. The homilist wishes to do his best and can find himself stretching the limits of legitimate theology to cover a death that is particularly tragic, or straining for novelty at a wedding.

Weddings and funerals are challenging too when you have a funeral in the morning and a wedding later the same day. Two very different moods are at work in the homilist as well as in the congregation, and it is not all that easy to switch emotional gears. We are challenged in supporting the bereaved and then in celebrating with the joyous couple and their families and friends, especially if either situation is nuanced, or delicate, for one reason or another.

The entire emotional event that is a wedding or a funeral impacts deeply and may be described as a significant homily in itself. It is a point worth keeping in mind when deciding on the length of our own homilies. In addition, the wedding ceremony is lengthy, and there will be speeches to follow at the reception. As for funerals, there are often tributes or someone else's eulogy at the end of the liturgy, and there is yet the graveside service to follow.

For these reasons, the homilist may wish to keep his homily

fairly short. All depends, of course, on the tradition of the place and on pastoral sensitivity to the particular circumstances at hand.

The value of a book of 'pre-packaged' homilies such as this one is a matter of discussion. Yet the books of homilies and homily hints keep on appearing, and every pastoral journal of note on both sides of the Atlantic has its homily section or homiletic notes. I think the discussion is fated to remain a dead-end one.

A more pertinent discussion would be the proper use of such books. Books of homilies are not written so that the homilist may read someone else's pages from his ambo – a not unknown marvel past or present! Nor are they written to douse, but to prime each individual homilist's own head and heart so they may produce their own unique compositions.

Homilists differ, and so do congregations. Books are written to encourage the homilist, and to offer him another angle, or a new idea, or an experience, or a story, or a line which may be the minor grace that gets him going – or that gets him past that block on the road.

Homilies For Weddings

Love seeks not itself to please,
Nor for itself has any care,
But for another gives its ease.

– William Blake, *Songs of Experience*

Readings: Ruth 1:16-17; 1 Cor 13:3-8, 13; Mk 10:2-9

For Terri and Robert: Believe!

And Pharisees came and to test him they asked, 'Is it lawful for a man to divorce his wife?' He answered them, 'What did Moses command you?' They said, 'Moses allowed a man to write a certificate of dismissal, and to divorce her.' But Jesus said to them, 'Because of your hardness of heart he wrote this commandment for you. But from the beginning of creation, "God made them male and female." "For this reason a man shall leave his father and mother and be joined to his wife, and the two shall become one flesh." So they are no longer two, but one flesh. Therefore what God has joined together, let no one separate.' (Mk 10:2-9)

Dear friends:

Today will be the most remembered day of your lives. Marriage and family life are the bedrock of the human race, the foundation on which we rest, the root from which we grow, and the place we find our home. Nothing can take their place. That's the way God set things up from the beginning, and he knew what he was doing. We read in the very first book of the Bible, 'Therefore a man leaves his father and his mother and cleaves to his wife, and they become one flesh.' (Gen 2:24)

Even though marriage is of God and the most natural thing in the world, it is a considerable risk. It is a risk at the best of times and a considerable risk today in our Western world. This is so, not so much because people are more selfish, but because life is more complex. Society is open, elastic, and traditional social institutions such as marriage are subject to much strain and questioning. If our church leaders are themselves 'unsure how to come to terms with the new pluralist society ... with other values and other voices' as John Ardagh says in his book *Ireland And The Irish*, should we be surprised if ordinary people are listening to these other values and voices and may question the value of the 'permanence and indissolubility' of marriage or lean towards the practicality of divorce for messy marriages that are 'broken beyond repair'?

Higher levels of education, greater personal freedom in decision making, the drive for self-determination, the questions raised by psychology as to the suitability of life-long commitments, the availability of jobs, and money in our pockets – all challenge old cautions and values such as life-long love and fidelity. They challenge the young couple whose beginning love is only a tender shoot looking for its light in the great canopy of the forest.

Against the backdrop of this shifting scene, I have one word for Terri and Robert: Believe! Believe in yourselves. Believe in your love. Believe in the durability of your love. Believe in the choice you have made of each other. Believe it is the best choice for you. Believe that God is in your decision, as he surely is, given your family pedigree and your own personal faith.

Believe that your love is just beginning, and that it will grow. It will grow as you work with it on a daily basis and as your daily priority. It will grow, and it will change in the growing, but the change will be to newer and different and deeper levels of love. Put your love of each other before all else in your lives. Don't think about the lifeboat when faced with the first challenge, nor about jumping ship at the first failure. Nothing in life comes fully developed at the start. What Ivor Kenny said of business leaders may be applied to lovers as well: 'One bit of experience essential to becoming a leader is failure. That is where there is real learning.' *(Leaders)* Or, as the writer and TV commentator Clive James puts it, 'Generally it is our failures that civilise us.' *(Unreliable Memoirs)*

Be understanding of one another, be flexible, be tolerant. That is the practical meaning of love. Ben Franklin, the American scientist and statesman wisely observed one time, 'Keep your eyes wide open before marriage; half shut afterwards.' *(Poor Richard's Almanack)* You are, in many ways, two different worlds coming together, and no synthesis, or union, is going to happen overnight or in a year, but through a lifetime spent together. And even after a lifetime spent together you'll each find yourself, in your old age, scratching your head on occasion and saying to yourself that the guy was right after all who said that men are from Mars and women from Venus!

And I have a word for you and me, the friends of Terri and Robert. By all means, let us give them all the good wishes and all the gifts that we can, but let us do something better: let us put Terri and Robert into our prayers. I'm afraid it's of little use these days to load young couples down with gifts, good wishes and a thousand toasts on this one great day of their lives and not lift them up in prayer every day. 'A successful marriage is an edifice that must be rebuilt every day,' writes André Maurois *(The Art Of Living)*, and prayer is one of its powerful building blocks.

Jesus says, 'I tell you whatever you ask in prayer, believe that you have received it, and it will be yours.' (Mk 11:24) 'More things are wrought by prayer than this world dreams of,' writes Tennyson in his *Idylls of the King*. The gospel of Luke tells us that 'Jesus told [his disciples]a parable, to the effect that they ought always to pray and not lose heart.' (Lk 18:1) Now I suppose all of us here agree with these statements and sentiments, but we can't imagine ourselves getting down on our knees every day and reeling-off endless rosaries in support of Terri and Robert.

But no one's asking for knee-bending and reels of prayer every day. Instead, just visualise Terri and Robert in your mind's eye and lift them up to the Lord now and then with a single line such as this scriptural prayer, 'Keep them, O Lord, as the apple of your eye; hide them in the shadow of your wings.' (Ps 17:8) We Irish do not pray enough for those we love while they live: we are always praying for them after they're gone. This is a strange inversion of the prayer priorities given by Jesus in the gospel.

Terri and Robert, our prayers are with you as you begin your married life through the vows you are about to exchange.

Readings: Tob 8:4-8; Col 3:12-17; Jn 2:1-11

For Deirdre and Gerry: A Sign Of His Concern

There was a wedding in Cana of Galilee, and the mother of Jesus was there. Jesus and his disciples had also been invited to the wedding. When the wine gave out, the mother of Jesus said to him, 'They have no wine.' And Jesus said to her, 'Woman, what concern is that to you and to me? My hour has not yet come.' His mother said to the servants, 'Do whatever he tells you.' Now standing there were six stone jars for the Jewish rites of purification, each holding twenty or thirty gallons. Jesus said to them, 'Fill the jars with water.' And they filled them up to the brim. He said to them, 'Now draw some out, and take it to the chief steward.' So they took it. When the steward tasted the water that had become wine, and did not know where it came from (though the servants who had drawn the water knew), the steward called the bridegroom and said to him, 'Everyone serves the good wine first, and then the inferior wine after the guests have become drunk. But you have kept the good wine until now.' Jesus did this, the first of his signs, in Cana of Galilee, and revealed his glory. (Jn 2:1-11)

Dear friends:

A wedding is a time of celebration. In the culture in which Jesus lived, wine was almost as commonplace as water. It was used in religious services, at festivals and on occasions of joy and celebration. And so, we find wine at the centre of the celebration called the wedding feast of Cana.

Deirdre and Gerry picked the wedding feast of Cana as the gospel reading for their wedding Mass. The three of us got together and went through it last week, and we want to share with you, our families and friends, what we came up with.

The wedding feast at Cana is a very human story. It is very down-to-earth. It's about the nuts and bolts of life. It strikes a responsive chord in our hearts. It tells of a human predicament, indeed the most embarrassing thing that could happen to a young couple on their wedding day: they run out of wine! Imagine all of us sitting at the Deirdre and Gerry's reception about two hours from now, and all our shocked faces, like death-masks, whispering to each other, 'Can you believe it, there're out of drink already!' Now that would be awful at any wedding. It would be a disaster at an Irish wedding.

But – if we Irish can imagine it to be possible – running out of wine at a Jewish wedding was actually worse than running out of drink at an Irish wedding. It was total disaster. And why? Because to run out of wine at a Jewish wedding was like running out of ice in the Arctic. It was simply unheard of. First of all, wine was commonplace in the Holy Land. Secondly, wine was a major sign of hospitality, of celebration, and of religious fellow-ship. Thirdly, wine was a symbol of the blood of the covenant between God and his people. Jesus, some time later, used wine at the Last Supper and said over it, 'This is my blood of the covenant, which is poured out for many for the forgiveness of sins.' (Mt 26:28) Wine was simply an essential presence at a Jewish event.

Mary, the mother of Jesus, notices the young couple's dilem-ma and she immediately moves to resolve it. After all, she is a mother and she was a bride herself in her day. She goes to her son and says simply, 'They have no wine.' She expects him to do something about it, and quickly. But he reacts in a way that sur-prises us. He hesitates. And when he speaks he addresses her as 'woman' rather than 'mother'. We are surprised at him because we are not thinking with his culture but with our own. 'Woman' meant 'lady' to him. It was a title of respect in public. In fact, we ourselves still use the word when we speak of Mary as Our Lady.

Jesus hesitates for a reason. He tells his mother that his hour has not yet come. He means that the time of his disclosure as the Messiah is not yet here, and so the time for working miracles, as approving signs of his Messianic mission, is still in the future. But his mother's intervention, and his own compassion, force him to work his first miracle ahead of schedule, so to speak, and in favour of the young couple on their wedding day. He changes water into wine for them. It is a wine of such superior quality that the marvelling steward says to the much-relieved bridegroom, 'You have kept the choice wine until now.'

Some people, down the generations, have felt that Jesus should have chosen a 'better' scene for his first miracle than a small wedding in a house in a country town; and that he should have chosen more 'socially significant' people as its beneficiaries rather than the young couple of Cana; and that he should have used a bigger stage for the purpose of more effective communication of his Messianic identity and his ministry. After all, he came as the Saviour of the whole world and with a gospel fit for all the nations of the earth and for all generations yet to be born. Why, then, did he choose such a poor launching pad for it all? Frankly, we don't know. All we can say is he chose what he chose, and his choice turned out to be a young couple, in a country town, on their wedding day.

The wedding at Cana has several lessons for me, and for Deirdre and Gerry, and for you. It tells us that young people, and married couples, and family life in general, rate high in the priorities of the gospel and in the love of Christ's heart and in the heart of his mother. Cana also tells us that the ordinary person is as important before the Lord as the most powerful personage of church and state; that the simple home is as important as the great palace or parliament building. Cana tells us that Mary is powerful with her son, as we would expect the good Jewish mother of a good Jewish son to be. Cana tells us to be confident when bringing our needs and our hopes to Jesus' mother so she may present them to her compassionate and accommodating son.

Cana was where Jesus gave, what our gospel writer calls, the first sign of his glory as the Son of God. He could have waited and chosen Jerusalem, God's city, rather than a country town, for his first sign. But he didn't. He could have waited and chosen the apostles as the beneficiaries of his first Messianic miracle. But he didn't. He chose what he chose, and it turned out to be a country wedding in a small town and a young couple starting off their married life together.

Deirdre and Gerry: Cana is a great and tender sign of the love of Jesus and his Blessed Mother for you, and for all young couples like you. Keep that in mind in the days ahead, and know where to turn in good times and in bad, in sickness and in health. Turn to Jesus, and turn to him through his tender mother.

Readings: Gen 2:18-24; 1 Cor 13:3-8, 13; Mt 22:35-40

For Monica and John: A Hymn Of Love

If I give away all my possessions, and if I hand over my body so that I may boast, but do not have love, I gain nothing. Love is patient; love is kind; love is not envious or boastful or arrogant or rude. It does not insist on its own way; it is not irritable or resentful; it does not rejoice in wrongdoing, but rejoices in the truth. It bears all things, believes all things, hopes all things, endures all things. Love never ends ... Faith, hope and love abide, these three; and the greatest of these is love. (1 Cor 13:3-8,13)

Dear friends:

The second reading of our Mass, from Paul to the Corinthians, is a favourite of John. It is called the great New Testament hymn of love. Usually, it's the bride who picks the readings with the love passages! But John has chosen this one.

I asked John why he favours this hymn of love. Very insightfully, he said he favours it because it describes what we ought to be doing in this world, and the only thing we'll be doing in the next world, and that one thing is love. Well said, John! We are built for love. We are less than human without it. And there is no such thing as a future called heaven without it.

Love is one of the words most often mentioned in the Bible and it is one of the divine and human activities most often described in it. And no wonder! John, the beloved disciple, said 'God is love, and he who abides in love abides in God, and God abides in him.' (Jn 4:16)

'All you need is love,' sang the Beatles one time when we were all a bit younger than we are now, 'love is all you need.' 'Love makes the world go round,' says an old anonymous French song. 'Love is the fulfilling of the law,' says the epistle to the Romans (13:10).

Love rules the court, the camp, the grove.
And men below, and saints above:
For love is heaven, and heaven is love.
(Sir Walter Scott, *The Lay of the Last Minstrel*)

Without love we do not grow, and die before our time. Why then, if love is so important, do we so often make a mess of it?

There are many reasons, I suppose. Some have to do with our personalities or with our arrested emotional development. We won't get into that here. Instead, we'll only note that if one looks – as I just did on the internet – at the lyrics of 500 pop songs from the 1950s to the present time one notices the dominance of a single, four-lettered word. That word is love. Even when we include the lyrics that are concerned with politics and peace and social awareness, we still find that the theme of these songs is love. We do, however, notice a shift as we move closer to our time. The lyrics begin to change from a dominantly other-centred and other-serving love to a slightly more self-centred and self-serving love.

Love often becomes as much a matter of what you and your love can do for me (e.g. 'help me make it through the night') as of what I and my love can do for you. Decades of people now in marriage, or just entering marriage, have listened to those lyrics and have been influenced by them, and by the shift from the dominance of love and concern for the other to considerable love of the self. Love, of course, does serve the self, but true love always emphasises the other. Is the shift one reason why there is much disappointment and frustration in modern-day love and marriage, and in expectations not being met? 'Love makes the world go round' for sure, but maybe we have weakened the other-loving, other-serving side of it and are suffering the consequences.

William Blake wrote:
Love seeks not itself to please,
Nor for itself has any care,
But for another gives its ease,
And builds a Heaven in Hell's despair.
('The Clod and the Pebble,' *Songs Of Experience*)

Robert Browning wrote, 'Such ever was love's way: to rise, it stoops.' *(A Death In The Desert)* God gave his only Son out of love for us and the Son, in his turn, gave his life out of love for us. Love is service of the other. 'I am among you,' said Jesus, 'as one who serves.' (Lk 22:27) Aldous Huxley, the promoter of man and nature over machine and system, wrote, 'There isn't any formula or method. You learn to love by loving – by paying attention and doing what one thereby discovers has to be done.' *(Time Must Have A Stop)*

'Love is patient,' says St Paul's hymn of love, 'love is kind. Love is not arrogant or rude, jealous or boastful ... does not insist on its own way ... is not irritable and resentful.' In other words, love is kind and considerate of the other. 'Love bears all things,' says St Paul. In other words, love is compassionate and consistently so. 'Love endures all things,' says St Paul. In other words, love shoulders for a lifetime the duties it signed up to, and all experienced married couples, God bless them, know that those duties can stretch you to the limit, not once or twice, but many times during the life of a marriage.

'What a recreation it is to be in love!' wrote George Colman, of love's power to renew us. *(Mountaineers)* 'Love me tender, love me true,' pleaded our old friend Elvis, expressing the gentleness and the sweet hope of love. 'How do I love thee? Let me count the ways,' wrote Elizabeth Barrett Browning in *Sonnets From The Portuguese*, 'I love thee to the depth and breadth and height my soul can reach.' She spoke here of her love of God of course, but all true lovers may speak her words to the spouse they uniquely love.

As many in this congregation know, love is renewing and tender and true and many-faceted, as all these poetic sentiments express, but true love must also be as tough as Swedish steel. True love has, as Robert Frost said of his own life, 'promises to keep, and miles to go before [it] sleeps.' *(Stopping by Woods on a Snowy Evening)* As you read through St Paul's hymn of love you see how all-embracing true love is and, therefore, how resilient and how durable it has to be as it meets all circumstances and moves through many years.

We should not be surprised that true love must be resilient and durable. No long-time married couple is. Still on the subject of love, St Paul tells us that, in the end, there are only three virtues that matter. These are faith, hope and love. And says Paul, 'the greatest of these is love.' Why did Paul say that? He said it because when we get to heaven faith and hope will be no more, for neither virtue will be needed there. Only love will remain, for love is what heaven is all about. God and we will be caught up in love's endless embrace. Love is the only thing that survives death and outlasts all time.

May Monica and John's love for each other be love as St Paul and all the poets describe it. May their love increase with the years. May it warm their hearts and their hopes and their home. May it be all good things to them in this life, and may it carry them into the everlasting joy of heaven where God, who is love, dwells with his beloved sons and daughters in endless love.

MARRIAGE OF A YOUNG COUPLE
Readings: Song of Songs 2:8-13; 1 Cor 13:3-8,13; Jn 15:12-16

For Mary and Kevin: May Your Store Increase!

The voice of my beloved! Look, he comes,
leaping upon the mountains, bounding over the hills.
My beloved is like a gazelle or a young stag.
Look, there he stands behind our wall,
gazing in at the windows, looking through the lattice.
My beloved speaks and says to me:
'Arise, my love, my fair one, and come away;
for now the winter is past, the rain is over and gone.
The flowers appear on the earth; the time of singing has come,
and the voice of the turtledove is heard in our land.
The fig tree puts forth its figs, and the vines are in blossom;
they give forth fragrance. Arise, my love, my fair one,
and come away.' (Song of Songs: 2:8-13)

Dear friends:
My grandniece Mary is, as you know well, a woman in a thousand! She is the real-life incarnation of vitality and vivaciousness. There is no end to her good humour or to her generosity or to her grace. She can charm birds from bushes, as the saying goes, and blossoms from the vine and fragrance from the flowers and maybe – if she were living in the Holy Land – even the coos from the turtledoves that are mentioned in the first reading of our Mass today.

Mary is full of life. She is a bubbling spring of laughter and lightness. The world seems to dance about her, and so does everyone entering her orbit. She makes all of us feel happy to be alive even on the most rain-sodden of Irish days. It's a remarkable grace, really, that God has gifted her with. I wish the world had a few million Marys so all people would see and experience the happy side of the God who made her and all of them in his own image.

21

Of course, she's not altogether perfect: no one is but God himself. Her great nature inclines her to a degree of extravagance. As you well know she's very gone on style and, as you also well know, her salary has never kept pace with her taste in clothes and her love of fashion. I assume Kevin knows this too. If he doesn't, he shouldn't be here this morning! At any rate, I trust my grandniece to have picked the right husband, for Kevin is not only a delight himself but a highly-salaried and most generous delight at that. Well done, Mary: you sure made the right choice! And bless you, dear Kevin, for not resisting your arrest when she handcuffed you with her love!

A few lines caught my eye recently which, for all the world, might be a scene from the future life of Mary and Kevin together. The scene shows a young married couple at home, and you can imagine Mary and Kevin in the lead parts:

> They had been married a year when the wife confessed that she'd splashed out his money on ten new pairs of shoes. 'Ten!' he exploded. 'What could you possibly want with ten new pairs of shoes?' She smiled at him fondly and said, 'Ten new handbags, dear.' (Barbara Jeffery, *Wedding Speeches & Toasts*)

Yes, that's our Mary alright, and that's her generous Kevin in the role of the accommodating husband!

When I officiated at the wedding of Mary's parents – in considerably poorer financial times, it may be said – I did for them what I did for all couples in those days: I gave them a list of the do's and don'ts of marriage according to the best marriage counsellors of the time. One hoped that this would be a help, and even serve as a small but sensible wedding gift as well. I remember some of the items on that list I gave your parents, Mary. They included open and honest communication; an ability at budgeting; the sensible use of alcohol; marriage first: friends second; and the binding value of family prayer.

I still believe that such lists are useful, if only to dispel the current notion that success or failure in marriage is mostly a matter of fate, or of how the tarot cards read, or the proper alignment of the stars in the sky on the day of your wedding. It's amazing how the present generation, so better educated, is so given to the idea of fate and luck. William J. Bausch (*A World Of Stories*) has a list of do's and don'ts which I came across recently and I'll pass it on here to the present generation. He thinks that you, Mary and Kevin, ought to be the following: you ought to be good chemists; bad mathematicians; humorists; realists; and pray-ers.

We often speak, these days, about the chemistry of a football team or the chemistry of a love relationship. When the chemistry is right, we say, everything works right. Then we speak of the chemistry being lost: the team doesn't gel anymore, the bubble of love deflates, the marriage goes flat. We speak as if we had no control over this chemistry – that it just happens in the first place and disappears in the second – but we have.

Chemistry is not magic; it is not fate; it is not a matter of the stars. Chemistry is something we ourselves create. That is why people in marriage need to be creative people. They have to mix the ingredients like a good chemist, or change them as needs be, to find the right prescription. They need to be creative enough to know when some aspect of the relationship is being overdone or underdone, when something needs to be changed or something new should be added, when a spot of therapy or of counselling might make scales fall from the eyes and renew the heart.

If it is important to be a good chemist in marriage, it is also important to be a bad mathematician. What Bausch means by this is that you shouldn't keep a scorecard. If God doesn't keep scores, why should we? Does God keep a scorecard? Listen to this from the scriptures: 'The Lord is merciful and gracious, slow to anger and abounding in steadfast love ... He does not deal with us according to our sins, nor requite us according to our iniquities.' (Ps 103:8,10)

Don't keep a scorecard. Put more into the marriage relationship than you wish to take out of it. Look out for #2 more than for #1. Do that, and you will discover the amazing truth of the Bible's words, 'Cast your bread upon the waters and it will come back to you after a time.' (Eccles 11:1) Jesus put that Jewish proverb another way when he said, 'Judge not, and you will not be judged; condemn not, and you will not be condemned; forgive, and you will be forgiven; give, and it will be given to you; good measure, pressed down, shaken together, running over will be put into your lap. For the measure you give will be the measure you get back.' (Lk 6:37-38) Be a good mathematician only in the area of budgeting.

Humour is important to a healthy marriage as it is to a healthy life. See the funny side of things, and be able to laugh at your own selves at least every now and then. And be realists for heaven's sake! You are not marrying an angel from heaven but another human being just like yourself. You are not marrying a person who is already perfect. Nor is your marriage supposed to be perfect just because you're in love and you're entranced by each other and you've made your own the lines of Ewan MacColl's haunting love song where the music expresses the lyric so beautifully:

The first time ever I saw your face
I thought the sun rose in your eyes,
And the moon and the stars were gifts you gave
To the dark and the end of the skies.
(The First Time Ever I Saw Your Face)

You are two independent beings, two different genders, two separate personalities, two 'others' working on the task of becoming one. It's a task that will take the length of your married life.

Finally, be pray-ers. I could make that request without raising an eyebrow in the past when we were all familiar with Fr Peyton's famous by-line, 'The family that prays together stays together.' Today, it's a different story. Such a suggestion seems to be beyond the radarscope and the psychology of a great part of present-day society. However, we should know that Bausch doesn't make the suggestion piously and only for a religious reason. He refers to a number of recent American psychological studies which favour prayer, and he quotes a Gallup survey to

the effect that 'happiness in marriage is better predicted by how
often a couple prays together than by how often they make
love.' *(A World Of Stories)* That, as Shakespeare has Hamlet say,
'must give us pause.' (Hamlet, 111)

May your love endure and grow, dear Mary and Kevin. May
your friends stand by you in good times and in bad. May you
never lose the love and the laughter and the lightness you share,
nor the grace and the joy that both of you are to all of us who so
dearly love you. May the Lord walk at your side all your days.

Readings: Gen 2:18-24; 1 Cor 13:3-8,13; Jn 15:9-12

For Nellie and Jer: Nothing Love Cannot Conquer

If I give away all my possessions, and if I hand over my body so that I may boast, but do not have love, I gain nothing. Love is patient; love is kind; love is not envious or boastful or arrogant or rude. It does not insist on its own way; it is not irritable or resentful; it does not rejoice in wrongdoing, but rejoices in the truth. It bears all things, believes all things, hopes all things, endures all things. Love never ends ... Faith, hope and love abide, these three; and the greatest of these is love. (1 Cor 13:3-8,13)

Dear friends:

We gather around Nellie and Jer in love and support as they begin their great voyage of discovery. The discovery we speak of is the many levels, the colours and the shades of this thing called exclusive love which they are solemnly pledging each other today. It takes a lifetime, no doubt, to uncover love's whole range, its weaknesses and its strengths, and to experience the ways in which these show themselves in the different stages of our lives.

St Paul, in our second reading, gave us some insights into the depth of the fulfilment, and yet the challenge and cost, of true love. Is such love a bridge too far for Nellie and Jer, for these two who are so young? Are they defying the odds and the wisdom of disapproving heads?

We have good reason to think not. You are surely as impressed as I by the manner in which Jer kept loving vigil by Nellie through her injuries, and through the long year of her recovery from her car crash. He kept loyal and loving vigil like a seasoned spouse. A lesser young man might have split, appalled by the injuries or by the prospect of what looked like a bleak future.

But Jer is no lesser young man. He proved to all of us what he is made of, and he confirmed for Nellie what she already knew instinctively of him and of their deep love. I, for one, am always genuinely delighted when the young disprove the caution of the old. The essayist Francis Bacon once wrote that, for those with faith and fortitude and love, 'adversity is not without comforts and hopes.' *(Essays)* 'Sweet are the uses of adversity,' wrote Shakespeare in *As You Like It,* and the greatest sweet that has emerged from Nellie and Jer's adversity must surely be the proving to each other and to us of their deep love.

Of the appalling carnage suffered by the British in a World War I battle, young Lieutenant J. R. T. Aldous wrote:

The tide ran in, that day, so deep

The sun was drowned; yet friendship flows

Deeper, from springs which childhood knows.

(Lyn Macdonald, *To The Last Man: Spring 1918*)

We do not know the measure of our faith and the depth of our love until they are severely tested. We do not know how strongly we believe and how truly we love until the tide runs in so deep the sun is drowned. It is then we know whether our faith and love are stronger than the drowning tide and able to withstand all adversity. It is, so often, the victims of great adversity who best understand faith and love and who really practise those great virtues. I am reminded of an incident told by William J. Bausch:

An unknown woman in Ravensbruck concentration camp wrote this little prayer and pinned it to the dead body of a little girl there. 'O Lord,' she wrote, 'remember not only the men and women of good will, but also those of ill will. But do not remember all the sufferings they have inflicted on us. Remember rather the fruits we have bought, thanks to this suffering: our comradeship, our loyalty, our humility, our courage, our generosity; the greatness of heart which has grown out of all of this. And when they come to judgement, let all the fruits which we have borne be their forgiveness.'

And Bausch adds:

Betsie Ten Boom, who died in the same concentration camp,

steadfastly refused to hate the guards who beat her and eventually beat her to death. Her dying words are both simple and profound: 'We must tell the people what we have learned here. We must tell them that there is no pit so deep that God is not deeper still.' *(A World of Stories)*

Adversity can bring out the best in us, and that is the story of Jer and Nellie. The pit was deep for Nellie and Jer but their love was deeper still.

Theirs is a great contemporary faith story and a great contemporary love story. It is a story that unfolded before our very faces here in this parish. It is the story of a love that might have weakened and died, but was challenged and grew. It is the story of a love that only grounded itself more securely in the face of adversity. 'Love bears all things,' says St Paul, and Nellie and Jer are his living proof.

May it be God's will, then, that the biggest cross Nellie and Jer have to bear as a couple has already been borne by them. May it be that nothing substantial threatens them or their home again. May it be that they live to great old age in the longest of married lives together!

Readings: Song of Songs 8:6-7; Col 3:12-17; Jn 2:1-5

For Sadhbh and Lorcan: Do Whatever He Tells You!

There was a wedding in Cana of Galilee, and the mother of Jesus was there. Jesus and his disciples had also been invited to the wedding. When the wine gave out, the mother of Jesus said to him, 'They have no wine.' And Jesus said to her, 'Woman, what concern is that to you and to me? My hour has not yet come.' His mother said to the servants, 'Do whatever he tells you.' (Jn 2:1-5)

Dear friends:

Most couples choose the wedding feast of Cana as the gospel for their marriage liturgy. It is easy enough to see why.

First of all, it involves Jesus at a wedding like yours today. Then it shows his very human side. He empathises with the young couple when they run out of wine and he saves them from embarrassment on their great day. And he makes available wine of such quality that the supervisor of the wedding feast says to the groom, 'You have kept the best wine for last.' And there is such an abundance of it too: six stone jars full – maybe 120 gallons in the estimate of the scholars!

St John, who recorded this gospel story, tells us that this incident of the changing of water into wine was Jesus' first public miracle. And he did it for a young couple just like Sadhbh and Lorcan.

'They have no wine,' says Mary out of her mother's heart. There are times in our lives when we have no wine. We should turn to Mary to find it for us. There will be times in marriage when you are stretched seemingly beyond your strength. There will be times as parents when you are at your wits' end and there is no answer to hand. You will have run out of the wine of energy or the wine of patience or the wine of insight. Turn to Mary. Tell her, 'We have no wine.' And be sure to be confident that she will direct you to where it can be found.

We are always running out of wine. There isn't enough time in the day; or when there is, we've run out of energy to use it all or to use it well. We plan to go on holidays with the whole family and the youngest suddenly comes down with asthma. We plan to replace the car in the new year with a bigger one to fit the growing family but the pipes burst in a hard December and we cannot stretch the finances. 'The best laid schemes o' mice an' men/ Gang aft a-gley,' said the Scottish poet Robert Burns. *(To a Mouse)* And we are not the only ones running out of wine. There is a whole world of the poor and the migrants and the marginalised out there who have no wine. 'They have no wine, nor peace, freedom, rights, food, housing, jobs, health ...' in the words of theologian Juan Alfaro (*Biblical Theology Bulletin* [1980], 14) but we can help them find it through our prayers and our support of the worthy causes and the servants that assist them.

When Mary first draws Our Lord's attention to the fact that the young couple have run out of wine, Jesus says something which surprises us. First, he addresses her as 'Woman.' That sounds cold and formal to us. But you will recall that Jesus addressed her in the same way from the cross. 'Woman, behold your son!' (Jn 19:26) 'Woman' means 'Lady'. It was the polite title that was given to a respectable woman in public.

Then he gives her what you and I might consider a sort of brush-off. He says, 'What has it to do with me?' One scholar (William Barclay) thinks it means the very opposite of how it sounds in English; he thinks it really means, 'Don't worry about it: leave it to me.' In other words, Our Lord will find a way to resolve the issue even though his appointed hour for working miracles has not yet arrived.

Well, you know what he did. He actually worked a miracle, ahead of his appointed schedule so to speak, and changed those six stone jars of water into high class wine. And he did it for a young couple, just like Sadhbh and Lorcan, on their wedding day.

Wine was not only a beverage to the Jewish people of old. It was a natural sacrament. It was a sign of joy – and even of grace.

It was, then, essential for Jewish feasts and celebrations. These could not take place without it. St John is telling us that Jesus did more than change water into wine at Cana, even into top quality wine: he made it possible for the feast to continue, he made it possible for celebration to continue, and he made joy abound.

I want you, Sadhbh and Lorcan, to take notice of Jesus and to turn to him in good times and in bad. Nothing in your love and in your marriage is beyond, or beneath, the concern of Jesus' great heart. Cana proves Jesus' great humanity, and Vatican II has this lovely passage to match it: 'He worked with human hands, he thought with a human mind, he acted by human choice, and he loved with a human heart.' (*Gaudium et Spes*, 22)

And take notice of his mother too. She is not only his mother but our mother, and she is your mother, Sadhbh and Lorcan. She has remarkable influence with her son as the Cana story shows us. 'My hour has not yet come,' he said. But she, knowing with her mother's heart the depth of her own son's humanity, said confidently to the servants, 'Just do whatever he tells you.'

'Do whatever he tells you.' This is Mary's way of showing us her confidence in her son on our behalf. 'Do whatever he tells you.' It is great advice. Mary is telling all of us to listen to the directing words of Jesus in the gospel and to do what they tell us to do. And if we all did, society's problems would substantially reduce and we ourselves would be saved untold disappointment, misery and heartbreak in our lives. But the trouble with Mary's advice is that many people do not heed it, or even know what Jesus is telling them. They are not in church to hear the word of God and they do not read the gospel of the Lord in their homes.

But such is not the case with you, Sadhbh and Lorcan. You are in church Sunday by Sunday, and I have given you a gilt-edged copy of the gospels as a wedding gift for your home so that you may listen to the Lord's directing words together, and later on, God willing, share them with your children in the heart of your home. For the home, not so much the parish, is the new frontline of the church.

Diarmuid Ó Murchú, a priest and social psychologist living in London, reminds us that we are not lone rangers on this planet. We depend on others for our growth and development as persons. 'I am at all times,' he writes, 'the sum of my relationships.' These relationships primarily involve people, but they also include what he calls our 'cultural ambience'. (*Evolutionary Faith*) I am suggesting to you, and to all of us, that our personal relationship with Jesus through prayer ought to be one of the critical relationships for our growth and development. And I am suggesting that our 'cultural ambience' – so heavily loaded with plain paganism these days and so much devoted to what is euphemistically called craic – badly needs the directing words of Jesus and the joy that comes from the new wine of his grace. We need to listen to him and to do what he tells us because he has our best interests at heart and because, as Ó Murchú points out, our usual notions about personhood and society are simply inadequate. If you follow the news stories of each day you'll see how real that inadequacy is.

May I ask you now, Sadhbh and Lorcan, to stand so you may exchange with each other the signs of your love and your marriage vows.

Readings: Gen 1:26-28, 31; Col 3:12-17; Jn 15:9-12

For Lynn and Darragh: Love Is Not Having To Look Back

[Jesus said], 'As the Father has loved me, so have I loved you; abide in my love. If you keep my commandments, you will abide in my love, just as I have kept my Father's commandments and abide in his love. I have said these things to you so that my joy may be in you, and that your joy may be complete. This is my commandment, that you love one another as I have loved you.' (Jn 15:9-12)

Dear friends:

The gospel we have just heard was spoken by Jesus at the Last Supper. It is part of his farewell message to his friends. It is his Last Will and Testament. He asks us to love one another as he has loved us. How did he love us? Totally. He loved us to the very end. This is his great commandment, his great teaching. The life of love is the life we are called to live. A life of loving, from the beginning to the end, is the life we strive to live in imitation of him.

The apostle John, in his First Letter, writes, 'This, remember, is the message you heard from the beginning: we should love one another.' (3:11 [NAB]) The Spanish mystic, St John of the Cross, said, 'In the evening of life we shall be judged on our love.' (*Dichos de Luz y Amor*, 64) St Thérèse, the Little Flower, observed: 'I understood that love comprised all vocations [including marriage], that love was everything, that it embraced all times and places.' (*Collected Letters*) From this day forward, Lynn and Darragh, your married life and your home is the time and the place of your life of love.

If love is everything, as Jesus and the apostle John and John of the Cross and the Little Flower say, why is it the cause of so much of our guilt? You know what I mean – parents looking back in their later years and saying, 'We should have done more for the kids'; the separated man or woman looking back in later life and saying, 'If I had done this or that I might have saved the marriage'; the old priest looking back from retirement and saying, 'I could have done so much better for the people and the parish.' That kind of looking back in guilt is the space between the rock and the hard place for people of my age. I would like to spare Lynn and Darragh such a prospect.

How do you love, then, in such a way that you don't have to look back later with guilt? I could quote you the therapists about not having over-expectations, sky-high ideals and false scripts, or I can introduce you to a little book I've just been reading. It's called *Hannah's Gift*.

Hannah's Gift is the story of a child who developed cancer the month before her third birthday and who died just before her fourth. The book is written by Hannah's mother, and here is the attention-grabbing first line of the first chapter: 'We both began bleeding on the same day.' The mother is bleeding because she is about to miscarry; little Hannah is bleeding because no one as yet knows that there is a fatal cancerous tumour filling her tiny stomach.

When Hannah's cancer is confirmed the doctor sits her parents down. What will he say to them at this shattering time? Well, he tells them that he is a parent himself and, remarkably, even as they speak his own two-year-old daughter is having a stem cell transplant at the Mayo Clinic in Minnesota in an effort to save her life. She has leukaemia. With that news, writes Hannah's mother, 'we went from a gathering of two parents and a doctor to two fathers and a mother who belonged to a club no one wanted to be in.'

The doctor speaks to Hannah's parents as himself the parent of a deathly-ill child, not as a paediatrician. He looks them in the eye and tells them calmly but ever so firmly, 'You are going to have to make thousands of decisions from now on that no one but the two of you can make; some of them may make a difference whether Hannah lives or dies. The best advice I can give you is this: Make the best decision you can with the information you have at that time.'

If you and I, and Lynn and Darragh, make our decisions the best we can on the basis of what we know at the time we make them, that is the best we can do in the circumstances and that is the conscientious decision and the loving decision. And that should be the end of it. There is, then, no need for sitting in the space between the rock and the hard place in the evening of our lives and looking back with guilt. We need not waste new time visiting old decisions when we made them after the manner of the doctor's advice. New time belongs to new challenges and new decisions, not to the past and its old decisions.

May I bless you, dear Lynn and Darragh, with that message? May all the decisions you make in your married life be made as best you can make them with the information you have at the time you make them. May you never have to look back on them except it be in quiet satisfaction and fond memory and with gratitude. Let me bless you and the decisions you will make in your married life with the same words that the priest Aaron used when he blessed God's people on their way to the Promised Land after years of wandering and wrong turns on the long road out of Egypt: 'The Lord bless you and keep you. The Lord make his face to shine upon you, and be gracious to you. The Lord lift up his countenance upon you, and give you peace.' (Num 6: 24-26)

MARRIAGE OF A YOUNG COUPLE
Readings: Tob 8: 4-8; Col 3: 12-17; Jn 15: 9-12

For Bláithín and Jim: May Your Joy Be Full!

[Jesus said], 'As the Father has loved me, so have I loved you; abide in my love. If you keep my commandments, you will abide in my love, just as I have kept my Father's commandments and abide in his love. I have said these things to you so that my joy may be in you, and that your joy may be complete. This is my commandment, that you love one another as I have loved you.' (Jn 15:9-12)

Dear friends:

Bláithín and Jim and their families welcome you to this liturgy of the celebration of their love. I think we all know that we are a small and select group of invitees here this morning. And I think we all know why.

A few years back, a niece of mine got married. She and her husband decided to do a very counter-cultural thing: they sat down and estimated the average cost of a wedding these days – and split the cost in half. They gave one half to good causes and the other half was spent on their wedding.

Jim and Bláithín have done the same thing today. I admire them for it. They have allowed me to disclose this fact only because I twisted their arms. I reminded them of the words of Our Lord to his followers, 'You are the light of the world. A city built on a hill cannot be hid. No one after lighting a lamp puts it under the bushel basket, but on the lampstand, and it gives light to all in the house. In the same way, let your light shine before others so that they may see your good works and give glory to your Father in heaven.' (Mt 5: 14-15). Bláithín and Jim are not blowing their own trumpet. I am blowing it because I feel that we are all encouraged and uplifted when we find young people doing what is Christian and counter-cultural in our quite worldly and greedy society. Miroslav Wolf, a Croatian theologian, notes that 'it is not a matter of indifference for Christians whether or not to be 'strangers' in their own culture. To the extent that one's own culture has been estranged from God [or Christ's values], distance from it is essential to Christian identity.' *(A Vision Of Embrace: Theological Perspectives on Cultural Identity & Conflict)*

I feel also, and so do many of you, that at the present time we've gone off the rails when it comes to what is spent on weddings, and even on children's baptisms, first communions and confirmations. In a sense, the sacraments are being submerged in money and partying. I feel that the decision of Bláithín and Jim in regard to the cost of their own great day is a present-day version of the lamp shining on the stand that Jesus called for. For word of what they have done will get around and, hopefully, light the way for others to follow.

Our generation seems to have gone off the rails too in its sense of celebration. It has a rake's sense, instead of a discriminating sense, of who and what is worthy of celebration and of how celebration should be done. Everything, good or bad, significant or trite, seems to be a cause for celebration. And celebration is not really celebration but so often just an excuse for partying, for getting drunk and going out of control. None of this makes any sense of course but, as Homer Simpson says to his wife in one TV episode, 'It's a party, Marge. It doesn't have to make sense.'

Anything – ordinary or holy – can be turned into an excuse for partying, into another excuse for the table to be spread for what Ernest Hemingway called the 'moveable feast' of our time. Our generation moves its table from party to party as though Alexander Pope had us in mind when he wrote, 'They shift the moving toyshop of their heart.' *(The Rape Of The Lock)*

Perhaps the toyshop heart has been draining the life out of our generation, spiritually speaking. It is a generation that believes it is cool and upscale, yet perhaps it has only been fattening itself on fantasy and escapes from real life and from real living. 'We had fed the heart on fantasies,' wrote Yeats of another generation, 'the heart's grown brutal from the fare.' *(Meditations In Time Of Civil War)*

Let us be clear on this: None of us is against celebration as such. None of us is opposed to a good party or a couple of drinks or joy or pleasure. Nor was Jesus. It's that we're in favour of moderation. And for a simple reason: In the final analysis, moderation is the key to enjoyment. Our hospital A&E units are very clear on this: You can have too much of a good thing.

Martin Luther said one time that to know the real Christ was not a matter of knowing the restrictions but of knowing the benefits. What are the benefits of knowing Christ? We learn from Jesus how to be human, and we see in Jesus our humanity properly defined and operating in his daily life. But many of our generation do not live their proper humanity because they do not really know Christ nor live out of their true hearts. Anthony de Mello tells this Hindu story:

One day God got tired of people. They were always pestering him, asking for things. So he said, 'I'm going away to hide for awhile.' He gathered all his advisers and said, 'Where should I hide? Where's the best place for me to hide?' Some said, 'Hide on the highest mountain peak on earth.' Others said, 'No, hide at the bottom of the sea; they'd never find you there.' Others said, 'Hide on the other side of the moon; that's the best place. How are they going to find you there?' Then God turned to his most intelligent angel and asked him, 'Where do you advise me to hide?' The intelligent angel smiled and said, 'Go hide yourself in the human heart. That's the only place where they never go!' (Walking On Water)

May all of us in this congregation bring a sense of Christian moderation to the moveable feast of our time. May we continue to avoid the toyshop heart and continue to live in – and from – our true human heart. It's the only heart we'll ever meet God in. And may we be encouraged in our living by the example of Bláithín's and Jim's moderation. And may the Lord, in turn, reward their counter-cultural stance with an abundance of his light and love and grace upon their future life together as wife and husband.

Readings: Song of Songs 2: 8-10; Eph 5: 2, 21-33; Mt 19: 3-6

For Deirdre and Liam: Walk In Love!

Live in love, as Christ loved us and gave himself up for us, a fragrant offering and sacrifice to God ... Be subject to one another out of reverence for Christ. Wives, be subject to your husbands as you are to the Lord ... Husbands, love your wives, just as Christ loved the church and gave himself up for her ... 'A man will leave his father and mother and be joined to his wife, and the two will become one flesh.' (Eph 5: 2, 21-22, 25, 31)

Dear friends:

Deirdre and Liam welcome you to this celebration of their love and of their future together as husband and wife. May it be a long and blessed one for them.

St Paul, or whoever stood in for him in writing the second reading we heard at this marriage liturgy, says something that makes him sound chauvinistic to modern ears and a bit out of touch. 'Wives,' he says, 'be subject to your husbands.'

Now that is a statement that upsets many women today. But, remember, it is only half of the sentence! The other half is, 'as you are to the Lord.' Wives should be subject to their husbands in the way all of us Christians are subject to Our Lord. And what way is that? It is the way of love. It is the way of love freely received and freely given. St Paul calls husbands to the same loving obedience in respect of their wives in verses 25-33 of this same reading. Paul calls no wife to slavery in the abject sense for he is the one who said that Christ has not given us 'a spirit of slavery' but 'the glorious freedom of the children of God.' (Rom 8: 15, 21)

As wives should be subject to their husbands in love so should husbands be subject to their wives in love. In fact, if Paul is tough on one gender more than the other in this epistle, it is not on the women but on the men! Why? Well, he demands of husbands something he does not demand of their wives. He demands that husbands love their wives even to the point of dying for them, if need be. He says, 'Husbands, love your wives as Christ loved the church, and gave himself up for her.' Paul does not make that same demand of wives. So there we are!

What Paul is trying to put before married couples in his Letter is, in fact, mainly the vision of a married couple fully in love and fully committed to each other as Christ is fully loving of us and committed to us. 'Walk in love,' says Paul, 'as Christ loved us.' Other versions of this same scripture read, 'Live in love, as Christ loved us' and 'Follow the way of love, even as Christ loved you.' All are saying the same thing: we should love one another in the manner Christ loved us and, if need be, to the point of death. This is a huge ideal and challenge for people in love. But it is possible, as all things are, with goodwill and God's enabling grace.

Such total love is, in fact, the kind of love that a really-in-love young couple have in mind and heart on their wedding day. Their love is so deep and so idealistic and heartfelt that they find nothing strange at all in Paul's challenging words. Quite the contrary; they are ready to take on the whole world, to eliminate all obstacles, even to move mountains, on behalf of the one they love!

Those of us who are priests easily resonate with Paul's words and with the idealism of young couples. Because on our ordination day we were so in love with Christ and with the prospect of ministering to his people that we were ready to live with him or die with him, to overcome all obstacles, to dig ditches or shift mountains, whatever he wished and whatever the ministry to his people asked of us. It is so great to be young, and to be so in love, and so full of the ideals of love! May you, dear Deirdre and Liam, follow the way of love, never lose your idealism, walk in love all your days, and live all your days in love.

I want to tell you a story that reflects this kind of enduring love. It's a story about the love which welds a married couple together, and has them living all their days in love, even into their declining years. It is a funny story, 'tis true, but it is also an engaging and a serious one as well. In the story the husband and wife are now very old and they have become very forgetful:

> He would forget where he put his eyeglasses. Then as he went from room to room searching for them, he would forget what he was looking for. She would announce that she was going to the shop for butter, but when she got there she would forget what she was shopping for. One evening, as they watched TV together, the husband stood up and the following dialogue took place:
>
> She: Where are you going?
>
> He: To get the snacks; it's my turn.
>
> She: I want a hot fudge sundae. Write it down!
>
> He: I don't have to write it down.
>
> She: And put nuts on it. Write it down!
>
> He: I don't have to write it down.
>
> She: And whipped cream on top. Write it down!
>
> He: I don't have to write it down.
>
> The husband then left to get the snacks. When he returned, he presented his wife with a plate of bacon and eggs. She looked at it and said, 'Where's the toast?' (William J. Bausch, *A World Of Stories*)

I do not intend this story, dear Deirdre and Liam, to be the script of a scene from your old age. It is not intended as an illustration of how forgetful things might be with the two of you in your distant future. It is, rather, a vignette which highlights the endurability and the triumph of married love and, God willing, of your married love. May long life be yours. May you grow old together and be as inseparable at the end as you are now at the beginning. And may you always 'live in love, as Christ loved us!' (Eph 5:2)

Readings: Gen 1: 26-28,31; Col 3: 12-17; Mt 7: 21, 24-27

For Joan and Art: Marriage As A Way Of Holiness

[Jesus said], 'Not every one who says to me, "Lord, Lord," will enter the kingdom of heaven, but only the one who does the will of my Father in heaven. Everyone then who hears these words of mine and acts on them will be like a wise man who built his house on rock. The rain fell, the floods came, and the winds blew and beat on that house, but it did not fall, because it had been founded on rock. And everyone who hears these words of mine and does not act on them will be like a foolish man who built his house on sand. The rain fell, and the floods came, and the winds blew and beat against that house, and it fell – and great was its fall!' (Mt 7: 21, 24-27)

Dear friends:

We gather around Joan and Art on their great day. Through their exchange of vows in this sacrament, they are sealing their love and establishing their home. You and I, their friends, wish to encourage them and to lift them up in prayer.

Jesus talks in the gospel about the importance of building your house on rock, on a solid foundation. The rock is love. God's directing words to us in the scriptures are some of the building blocks, and his grace is the cement.

There is much discord in marriage and in the home today. I don't mean the ordinary bumps and scrapes of family life, but big fractures. It seems that we're finding it harder than ever to live together in marriage. Has it anything to do with the lack of God's law in our personal lives as we grow up and the lack of good manners and courtesy in the homes we come from? Has it anything to do with expecting too much of the other? Has it something to do with impatience and the lack of tolerance, forgiveness and trust? Do we need to dedicate our homes to the Lord as our steady grandparents of yesteryear dedicated their homes to the Sacred Heart?

Just before Joshua led the Hebrews into the Promised Land, into the national home that God had promised them, he gathered all the tribes and urged them to renew their covenant with God. He tried to encourage them with the words you often see on a plaque in American homes: 'As for me and my house, we will serve the Lord.' (Josh 24: 15) Those words should be words of meaning in our Christian homes, and words of blessing upon our homes. 'As for me and my house, we will serve the Lord!'

Marriage is a way of holiness. That's an old Christian idea which is likely these days to be met with a chuckle or a comment such as, 'Man, what planet are you living on?' But we need to say it again to ourselves because we are Christians: marriage is a way of holiness. In fact, it is most people's way to holiness! If most people are ever going to be saints it will be in and through their marriages.

In talking about marriage as the union of two bodies and not just of two souls, St Josemaría Escrivá says, 'No Christian ... has a right to underestimate the value of marriage.' (*Christ Is Passing By*) In context, he means that marriage has great spiritual value, and that value specifically is marriage's ability to develop holiness in married people.

Marriage, and what it requires of a couple, is the stuff of sanctity. For the road of marriage is not an always smooth one. The humorist James Thurber once wrote the following to some friends about his own marriage: 'We are an ideal couple and have not had a harsh word in the seven weeks of our married life.' (*Selected Letters*) I wonder what he wrote after seven years! Marriage requires patience and trust and tolerance and forgiveness if it is to travel farther than just seven weeks, as all of you married experts in this congregation well know.

William Bausch quotes a famous writer, Madeline L'Engle, on her relationship with her husband during a forty-three year marriage:

> Our love has been anything but perfect and anything but static. Inevitably there have been times when one of us has outrun the other, and has had to wait patiently for the other to

catch up. There have been times when we have misunder-
stood each other, demanded too much of each other, been in-
sensitive to the other's needs. I do not believe there is any
marriage in which this does not happen. The growth of love
is not a straight line, but a series of hills and valleys. I suspect
that in every good marriage there are times when love seems
to be over. Sometimes those desert lines are simply the only
way to the next oasis, which is far more lush and beautiful
after the desert crossing than it could possibly have been
without. *(A World Of Stories)*

William Bausch notes that the findings of some recent American
marriage surveys may surprise us. For example, prayer plays a
major role in determining how a couple regard each other; religion and spirituality play a major role in marriage happiness;
and 'decades of research have demonstrated that people highly
involved in their faith have the happiest marriages.'

The sacrament of marriage gives the couple the grace they
need to maintain their love and to live in unity, to build their
home and to sanctify it. It even gives them, says the *Catechism of
the Catholic Church*, the grace 'to attain holiness in their married
life.' (#1641) Therefore, I can confidently tell Joan and Art that
the sacrament, which they are now about to administer to each
other, will do just that for them. God be with them on their journey to their promised land!

Readings: Jer 31: 31-34; Rom 12: 9-21; Mt 5: 1-12

For Sorcha and Brian: Until We Come To It

We, this people, on a small and lonely planet
Travelling through casual space
Past aloof stars, across the way of indifferent suns
To a destination where all signs tell us
It is possible and imperative that we learn
A brave and startling truth ...
We, this people, on this wayward, floating body
Created on this earth, of this earth
Have the power to fashion for this earth
A climate where every man and every woman
Can live freely without sanctimonious piety
Without crippling fear
When we come to it
We must confess that we are the possible
We are the miraculous, the true wonder of this world
That is when, and only when
We come to it.
(Maya Angelou, *A Brave and Startling Truth*)

Dear friends:
Sorcha and Brian have included Maya Angelou's poem, *A Brave and Startling Truth,* in their wedding booklet. It is their favourite poem. It speaks very much to their hearts and to the work they do. The poem was composed for the 50th anniversary of the founding of the United Nations and delivered there by the author. I encourage you to read the whole poem and to reflect on it. I know that Sorcha and Brian would consider your reading of that poem and your reflection on it as the best wedding gift you could give them.

Sorcha and Brian are an unusual couple in this age and, indeed, in any age. They are admired by all of us. That is why we have gathered around them in love and support on their wedding day. We love them for their love of the poor and for their commitment to justice and peace and the building of a better earth. We admire them for their years of social work on behalf of the least of Christ's sisters and brothers in our city, dragging themselves at all hours through the streets and alleys in response to human need, and being subjected on occasion to abuse and assault even from those they serve. This is their fulltime life – almost a homeless life – and they have been living it for a long time now and are committed to continuing it. May God be always with them down the years, and on the streets and in the back alleys.

Hands-on hardcore social work cannot be an easy job for them. But, then, it's no job to them: it's the vocation they feel called to in the very marrow of their bones. This is a time when Ireland's ideals have gone corporate, and when Sorcha and Brian's peers are climbing the economic ladder and planning to settle down in state-of-the-art homes in the suburbs while they themselves are out-of-pocket and out of social standing because of their dedication to God's kingdom of love and peace and justice in our city.

I first heard Maya Angelou speak at a religious education congress in California a few months after her UN visit. Her poem is a vision for our world, for a world living in harmony, in love and justice and peace.

We will come to it, she says magnificently, we will come to such a world when we take up peace-making as the priority and with all our energies engaged in the task. Then we will arrive in a world where the great ideals of the ages have become reality. We will come to this new world only when we have worked hard for it. We will come to it because a generation finally decided not to leave it sitting there merely as someone's lovely blueprint in a lovely book or manifesto. We will come to this new world when we ourselves have made it so.

There are things to be done which are part of the process of coming to that renewed world. We will come to it because we finally opened our hostile fists and allowed 'the pure air to cool our palms'. We will come to it because we finally let the curtain fall on 'the minstrel show of hate', and ceased to hide behind our faces scornful of others. We will come to it because we stopped allowing battlefields and political power games 'to rake our unique and particular sons and daughters up with the bruised and bloody grass to lie in identical plots' in early cemeteries all over the world instead of in cemeteries at home at the end of a long and productive and loving life.

We will come to it when we have abandoned the all too common form of religion that is nothing more than pious cant and money gathering, and when we have abandoned attacks on the old and the young, and when 'childhood dreams are not kicked awake by nightmares of abuse' anymore, and when we have silenced our 'cankerous words' and replaced them with 'songs of exquisite sweetness'. We will come to it when we know that the wonder of our world is found not only in the mystery of the great Pyramids' mathematical precision and in 'the Grand Canyon kindled into delicious colour by western sunsets', but also in these hands of ours which 'can touch with such healing, irresistible tenderness.'

We will come to it when we realise that we ourselves have the power to make real the ideal world, and when we humans confess that it is ourselves who are 'the possible' and 'the miraculous,' and 'the true wonder of this world'.

You may notice that she makes no reference to God or to his Son's kingdom in her poem. She makes no reference to Christ or to his enabling grace. Her poem is addressed to all nations and all peoples and all cultures and all religions in the family of man. Nevertheless, her vision for a world of love and peace and justice is eminently parallel to God's plan and Christ's kingdom.

Perhaps she assumes that God and grace are not what we lack but a new belief and vigour in our own hearts whereby birth is given to the new world. It is we that the new world depends on in order for it to be born. It will not come about without us. Without our converted heart, grace is always stymied.

The emphasis has to be on our hearts, our efforts, our co-opera-
tion and our goodwill.

Maya Angelou's vision for the world is Sorcha's and Brian's
vision for Irish society and for our city, and fanning out from
those like ripples in a pond, for the whole world at large. May
the same vision be ours as well. Above all, may we have the
heart to put ourselves behind the vision and to push for it in our
own time and place. We may feel puny in the face of the seemingly massive task of transforming this fractured and forever
fighting world of ours into one of reconciliation and love and
peace and justice. But each of us is needed in the task, each of us
is critical to the new world's becoming, and it will not be born
without us, and it will not be born at all until it is first born freely
within each of us.

We can help make it happen. For the world of which we
speak is each one of us and the sum of all of us. John Donne
wrote, 'No man is an Island, entire of itself: every man is a piece
of the Continent, a part of the main.' (*Devotions*, 17) Pablo
Picasso once said, 'Every human being is a whole colony.' (Gilot
& Lake, *Life With Picasso*) And St Paul wrote, 'We are members
one of another.' (Eph 4:25)

You and I help to make the new world happen through the
love and the peace and the justice we bring into our own hearts,
into all of our relationships, and into the daily world we inhabit.
The daily world we inhabit is the relatively small world of influ-
ences and relationships that revolves around us every day.
Every married couple helps the new world become a reality
through the way they respect and treat each other. Each small
family helps the new world happen through what happens in
love and sharing and forgiveness within the confines of the
home. For the world of Maya Angelou, her vision of our future,
depends on the 'brave and startling truth' that the world in
question is the human world and that it is no greater or lesser
than the aggregate of the good hearts of all the individuals and
families on earth.

It is in that sense that we are all involved in the great vision, so that when Angelou sees her future world made real she is relying on people like Sorcha and Brian and you and me, dear friends, to be its building blocks and its binding mortar. May Sorcha and Brian continue their great work, and may their love and marriage only add to it and sustain and strengthen them together.

Readings: Gen 2: 18-24; Rom 15: 1-6; Jn 2: 1-10

For Phyllis and Jim: The Best Wine Now

There was a wedding in Cana of Galilee, and the mother of Jesus was there. Jesus and his disciples had also been invited to the wedding. When the wine gave out, the mother of Jesus said to him, 'They have no wine.' And Jesus said to her, 'Woman, what concern is that to you and to me? My hour has not yet come.' His mother said to the servants, 'Do whatever he tells you.' Now standing there were six stone jars for the Jewish rites of purification, each holding twenty or thirty gallons. Jesus said to them, 'Fill the jars with water.' And they filled them up to the brim. He said to them, 'Now draw some out, and take it to the chief steward.' So they took it. When the steward tasted the water that had become wine, and did not know where it came from (though the servants who had drawn the water knew), the steward called the bridegroom and said to him, 'Everyone serves the good wine first, and then the inferior wine after the guests have become drunk. But you have kept the good wine until now.' (Jn 2:1-10)

Dear friends:

We gather here with dear Phyllis and Jim to celebrate their love and to wish them many blissful years together.

The fact that their wedding day comes late in their lives does not mean that love has come late in their lives. Not at all. As you know, they have been dating a long time. In fact, when they started it was still called 'doing a line' and Bono and the boys of U2 were just beginning to put their great act together in a secondary school in Dublin! I know that Phyllis and Jim will not misunderstand my words when I tell them that all of us have the utmost confidence in their marriage precisely because they have been getting ready for it for so long!

At any rate, age is no measure of true love. Age is said to be a state of mind. In many ways, it is. Age is mostly a matter of how you look at it. When I was very young I thought every man in his mid-forties was the ancient mariner. You could see lines on his face that told you he had weathered many a summer and many a winter. Now I look at men in their mid-forties and only see the baby boomers who arrived after my own best years. I see these men now as fresh faces, veritable youngsters, fit enough to fight a war or shoot a round of golf in the low seventies on a windy day.

Much the same thing has happened to me with respect to women. There used to be two classes of women for me: girls and all the others. Now I have to mind my manners in the shop so I don't say 'good girl yourself' to the middle-aged woman with the expensively exfoliated face and the flaming hair who serves me with a smile deferential of my age.

I was watching *Ros na Rún* some time ago – just to keep in touch with what's supposed to be happening in the Irish-speaking world, mind you! – when two fairly young things made a couple of comments about love between two older things. One of the young things was put-off by the idea of love between the older things while the other one said philosophically, 'Love is love at any age.' Indeed, it is. And I think that love may be more settled and seasoned, like great wine, when it has aged in the arms of an older couple. (cf Sir 9:10)

In our gospel reading, our attention is drawn to the fact that the best quality wine is said to be served at the start of a Jewish wedding reception and the wine of lesser vintage is said to be served when the guests 'have drunk freely' and are less able to appreciate the difference. I don't think that Our Lord's words infer that the guests were actually drunk, for 'drunkenness was in fact a great disgrace,' says William Barclay, and orthodox people, such as the guests at the wedding feast of Cana, 'actually drank their wine in a mixture composed of two parts of wine to three parts of water.' (I'm telling you this technicality so you'll know why no Irish guests showed-up at the wedding feast of Cana!)

In the time of Our Lord and in a country where wine was used at every meal, there could never be more than a small quantity of high quality wine available to ordinary people. In this scenario, it was only proper that the best wine be served first at weddings while it could be best appreciated. No doubt the best wine was served first at Cana in accordance with this custom – but the striking thing to the guests at Cana was that an even better wine was served last!

In any event, Jesus works his first public miracle in favour of this couple on their wedding day. He changes water into wine for them because they've run short and public humiliation threatens them on their great day. The wine steward, not knowing where this high quality wine has come from, is so impressed that he says to the bridegroom, 'You have kept the best wine for last.'

In keeping with the theme of our gospel, all of us here say to Phyllis and Jim: You have drunk the good wine of your courtship over many years. Now may the love of the years of your married life together be the best wine kept till last.

Readings: Song of Songs 8: 6-7; Eph 4: 1-6; Mk 10: 6-9

For Heather and Tony: Surprised By Love

Set me as a seal upon your heart,
as a seal upon your arm;
for love is strong as death ...
Many waters cannot quench love,
neither can floods drown it.
If one offered for love
all the wealth of his house,
it would be utterly scorned. (Song of Songs 8: 6-7)

Dear friends:
Performing this wedding ceremony for Heather and Tony is not a pastoral duty for me but a personal delight. Tony and I go back a long way, to national school in fact, and most of the water of our lives has already flowed under our bridges. Be that as it may, life is for living and not for looking back, and today is a high water mark in the lives of Tony and Heather and, indeed, in my own life too because I am overjoyed for them and with them.

When Tony's dear wife, Margie, died in 1998 he found himself all alone in London. It was a whole new experience for him. It was not what he expected in life, and it was not what he wanted. Tony and Margie were not blessed with children so there was no close support, no support of the same flesh and blood, in his life. He found out the truth of God's word that it is not good for man to be alone. (See Gen 2:18)

Fortunately, or I should say blessedly, Heather was a God-send. Because of Heather everything came together for Tony. Tony speaks of the support and the grace and the healing force that Heather has been in his life of recent years. She is the love that has lifted him up, renewed his spirit, and it is right and fitting that their love has blossomed into the beauty and into the commitment of this marriage day.

As for Heather, she had more or less given up on finding her knight in shining armour as the years passed and the bruising anonymity and suspicious nature of big city London life increased. Besides, her time and her energies moved away from the romantic path and increasingly centred themselves on her nursing profession and on the elderly people who had come to rely on her care. In any event, she was surprised when love came calling in the form of Tony, and even more surprised when she found herself unable to keep the door of her heart closed against his sensitivity and his goodness and his love. May God be praised that they found each other, and may he be thanked for his concern and guidance in both their regard.

People sometimes wonder about two people falling in love in their later years. I think they are only wasting their time wondering about it. It happens. Thank God it does. And that's that! Love is unpredictable, and love at any age is a wonderful discovery and a great blessing. It is never too late to find love and to be loved uniquely.

I spoke one time in California at the first Mass of a student of mine. He was older than myself in fact, and had lived a long life already as a union organiser and, later, as a labour arbitrator. I knew that some of his old buddies were surprised when he entered the seminary and, even more so, when he persevered. They wondered if his age was against him and if he would even have as many years in ministry as he spent going through the seminary formation programme. The point of my talk was to stress that the quality of whatever years we are given by God is more important than the number of them.

In the same way, it is not the number of years in marriage that really counts but the love that shapes and fulfils whatever number the years are. Robert Browning noted that the purpose of a long or a short life is the same: it is 'the chance of learning love.' (*A Death In The Desert*) If the purpose of life is the chance of learning love, surely the joy of life is the experience of it.

We listened to the following lines in the first reading which Heather chose for her marriage liturgy: 'Set me as a seal upon your heart, as a seal upon your arm.' These lines are from the Song of Solomon, the Bible's Song of Songs. Heather wishes to make these lines her own and she speaks them to her beloved Tony. What do they mean?

In biblical times, a person's commitment to another person in a business matter was guaranteed by the use of a seal. It was not the person's word or signature that mattered so much as the person's seal. The seal represented your whole person, your entire being standing behind it. Heather wishes to be sealed on Tony's heart, impressed on his arm. Heart and arm stand for love and protection. When someone is sealed on our heart and on our arm it means that we undertake to love and protect that someone in a unique and exclusive way. In Tony's case, Heather is the one to be loved uniquely and protected exclusively. And, of course, in Heather's case, Tony is the one to be exclusively loved and supported by her. They are, from now on, a seal on each other's heart and arm.

Dear Heather and Tony: The years ahead for you may be many years or less than many. I feel it doesn't really matter all that much. To love intensely and to be loved intensely is what matters. Such love so touches the centre of us that even a moment of such love is an enduring satisfaction. Remember, then, the primacy of quality over quantity, and of true love over time. What matters for you is that you found each other, and that you've found a quality of love that seals each of you to the other as exclusive delight and joy. What matters in any worthwhile human life is to experience, even for a moment, the dynamism of such a love.

A CULTURALLY MIXED MARRIAGE
Readings: Ruth 1: 16-17; Col 3:12-17; Mt 19: 3-6

For Leslie and Michael: A New Identity

Ruth said, 'Where you go I will go; where you lodge I will lodge; your people shall be my people, and your God my God. Where you die, I will die – there will I be buried. May the Lord do thus and so to me and more as well if even death parts me from you.' (Ruth 1: 16-17)

Dear friends:

For many centuries we were known as a nation of emigrants. Thank God the tide has turned in our time.

At first, Irish emigration was mainly a matter of Irish monks going out and traversing the known world and bringing the light of the gospel to the people who walked in darkness, especially after the so-called Dark Ages in Europe.

These were followed by other Irish emigrants, such as the dreamers and the adventurers and the seekers of fortune and the servants of various employments. But it is the Famine that really made us emigrants *en masse* and that gave the word emigration the horror it has had in the Irish psyche until the arrival of the four-engined jet and the global village.

Now Irish history has reversed itself. We have become a nation of little emigration but of considerable immigration; fewer of us are leaving our shores but more of other nations are reaching them. They wish to become a part of us. We should welcome them, and appreciate the honour they do us. But we must respect their basic autonomy and rights and their cultural traditions and not make false 'melting pot' demands of them. None of the countries to which Irish emigrants went in the past made false demands of them – as people such as myself well know and remember gratefully. Christ calls no one to be the victim of anyone else's overlordship, or to be precise and identical ingredients coming out of any nation's 'melting pot'.

And while we're on the subject! – let us not judge the new immigrants by those who abuse the system, for we had our share of abusers in our own emigrant times. For instance, the Commissioners For Emigration in Liverpool had to continually warn the poor Famine Irish en route to America and Canada against a glut of con men 'many of them originally from their own country and speaking their native language.' (Edward Laxton, *The Famine Ships*)

In the first reading of our liturgy we heard lines from the Old Testament Book of Ruth. They are lovely lines. Ruth says, 'Where you go I will go; where you lodge I will lodge; your people shall be my people.' (Ruth 1:16) Ruth says, 'Your people shall be my people.' It is her free choice. She chooses to become part of another family and part of another nation.

'Your people shall be my people,' said Ruth. The words are especially fitting for Leslie in her marriage to Michael because, as all of us know, she came here from somewhere else. She came from another country, and we are so glad that she did. No one is more glad than her beloved Michael. Ruth spoke her lovely words when her husband died. She spoke the words to Naomi, her mother-in-law. Ruth could have chosen to go back to her own Moabite people after her husband's premature death, but she didn't. She chose instead to become part of another people, Naomi's people, the Jewish people. So she said to Naomi, 'Where you go I will go; where you lodge I will lodge. Your people shall be my people.'

Ruth spoke her words freely. Leslie has chosen the lovely lines of Ruth for the first reading of our Mass, and she is making her own statement by means of them. She will go where Michael goes. She will lodge where he lodges. She will take his name, the name of his people. She will have a new identity. And this is entirely the way she wants it.

The lines of Ruth, which Leslie has made her own, may sound old-fashioned but they are not subservient. If anything, they lay a greater charge on Michael that he love her and cherish her all their days. And he is more than happy to promise that cherishing because he knows the depth of the love and of the commitment that underpins the lovely lines of Ruth which Leslie has made her own and speaks to Michael today in her love of him.

Ruth's choice turned out to be a happy one. Her lines turned out to be blessed lines. She became the great-grandmother of King David and it was from David's line that our Messiah, Jesus, was born. May Leslie's choice and the lines she has made her own be full of blessings for her too.

And what of us, you and me, the friends of Leslie and Michael? Where do we fit into the lessons of the Book of Ruth, and in what sense are we ourselves able to speak the lovely lines she spoke?

The Book of Ruth – and particularly the lovely lines she spoke – is a teacher of tolerance. In their day, the lovely lines of Ruth helped to create something unusual in the traditionally closed Hebrew society: they helped to create an understanding of and acceptance of foreigners. The Book of Ruth, and her lovely lines, are a template of tolerance as later, in the Christian era, were the words of the Rule of St Benedict: 'Let thoughtful care be had for the reception of strangers from afar; for in these do we most truly welcome Christ.' Leslie and Michael in their married union are a template too. They challenge you and me to be people of tolerance in a nation of tolerance. 'Make space for the other in the self, and rearrange the self in the light of the other's presence' (Miroslav Wolf, *World of Exclusion, Vision of Embrace*) instead of presuming that the other must always fit the mould we make for them.

Marriage itself is the great teacher of tolerance because it is the great teacher of true love. As Leslie and Michael begin their journey of love and tolerance together, we bless them and we wish them long life and every happiness. And we affirm their union, forged as it is out of two different nations and cultures, by calling down a blessing upon ourselves. It is this: May we deepen love in our Irish society by cherishing each other's differences and welcoming the foreigners who choose to come and live among us. Theirs, too, is the story of Ruth, the story of choosing to become part of another people, to go from this time forward where we go, to lodge from now on where we lodge, to make us their people, even to await the resurrection in burial places beside us.

None of this is a threat to us. All of it is an honour. And, as we learn from the Book of Ruth, it is also a blessing.

Readings: Ps 128; Eph 4: 1-6; Mt 19: 3-6

For Una and Alan: Covenant Love

Happy is everyone who fears the Lord, who walks in his ways.
You shall eat the fruit of the labour of your hands;
you shall be happy, and it shall go well with you.
Your wife will be like a fruitful vine within your house;
your children will be like olive shoots around your table.
Thus shall the man be blessed who fears the Lord.
The Lord bless you from Zion!
May you see the prosperity of Jerusalem all the days of your life!
May you see your children's children.
Peace be upon Israel! (Ps 128)

Dear friends:

As we gather to celebrate the wedding of Una and Alan, we especially welcome Alan's parents, his sisters and brother, and his friends to our church. What binds all of us together, apart from Una and Alan, is our common baptism as Christians and our commitment to the Lord Jesus as the master of our lives and destiny. To him be praise now and forevermore!

The first reading we heard today is Psalm 128. It was the lesson read at the wedding of June and Adrian, Alan's parents, twenty-eight years ago in Cowes on the Isle of Wight. May it be as fruitful a lesson for Una and Alan as it has been for them.

Marriage, as you know, is a tough undertaking at the best of times. It is all the more challenging now in this time of questioning, this time of lesser societal support for Christian marriage, and this time of short-term contracts and commitments which tend to alter the psychology that shapes our values and our commitments.

According to received wisdom, marriage is additionally challenged when it is undertaken by a man and a woman of different religious persuasions. On the other hand, may I say that many of the most stable marriages I have been honoured to witness as a priest have been marriages such as this so-called 'mixed marriage' which Una and Alan are now entering.

I find these marriages to be especially stable when both parties are committed Christian believers, as Una and Alan are; when they understand that their marriage is fully a sacrament despite the different denominations they belong to, which Una and Alan do; and when they realise, with St Paul, that the marriage of two Christians – of whatever denomination – is an image of Christ's union with his bride, the church. (cf Eph 5:32)

Dear Una and Alan, you are not uniting together today on the basis of our culture's conditional understanding of marriage: you are marrying 'in the Lord'. You are marrying on the basis of your own faith, and on the basis of your exclusive love for each other, and on the basis of Christ's abounding grace supporting what you are doing together and given to you in this Christian sacrament.

In the Bible marriage is not only a normal human relationship; it is the vocation of most people. And it is the creation of God. It is meant to be something joyous and fulfilling. Gradually, in the pages of the Bible as they reflect the passing of the generations, rules and regulations enter the marriage scene. There are restrictions as to marrying close blood relatives. There are regulations with regard to hereditary rights and property. There is a decree against marrying foreigners after the chosen people return from their bitter Babylonian captivity. There is even an allowance of several wives for the king during the period of the monarchy.

As time further passes, there is lesser moral condemnation for the unfaithful husband than for the unfaithful wife. Even a writ of divorce is introduced – mainly in the man's favour. Jesus later says that this writ came about because of man's 'hardness of heart' rather than as a marriage ideal or by the permission of God. (Mk 10: 5) Yet, through all of this history, the ideal of marriage as an exclusive and lifelong arrangement between two believers, and in the presence of their God, is retained.

The ideal of marriage as an exclusive and lifelong arrangement is not based, then, on something aerie-faery, nor on the musing of some holy man or prophet of the desert, nor on the assumption of the sociologists that it was necessitated by the need of nurturing children in a time when adult lifespans were short. It is, rather, based on the nature of the sacred covenant that God made with his people. The covenant bound God to his people and the people to God as though they formed a married couple. The covenant was sacred, it was exclusive, and it was permanent.

We see this idea of the covenant as a marriage bond between God and his people in a number of scriptures, for example, in Psalms 105 and 106. Psalm 105 recites the events by which God fashioned the nation of Israel, and Psalm 106 recounts all God's fidelities and Israel's many infidelities. Despite the love of the one partner and the lack of it on the part of the other, God remains faithful to his covenant love. 'They defiled themselves by their deeds and broke their marriage bond with the Lord.' (106: 45)

Our spiritual ancestors, these Hebrews, came to believe that the marriage of two God-fearing people, such as you, Una and Alan, is similarly sacred, exclusive, and permanent. Married love is 'a seal upon the heart' to match the sealing of God's covenant with his people in blood. Married love is a love 'strong as death' that 'many waters cannot quench nor floods drown' (Song of Songs 8: 6-7) as is the eternal love between God and his covenanted people.

It is this covenant theology of marriage, upheld in his turn by Jesus, that you accept and that you offer each other, and that I witness to today in this sacrament. May your covenant endure, and your love only deepen, in the passage of the days and the years of your married lives together.

Homilies for Funerals

Death is an event that begs for
spiritual guidance and context
perhaps even more piercingly
than it calls for medical science's assistance.

– Dr Kathleen Dowling Singh, *The Grace In Dying*

DEATH OF AN OLDER PERSON

Readings: Jer 1: 9-10, 15:16; Rom 14: 7-12; Jn 5: 24-29

Teresa
(who loved the word of God)

The Lord put out his hand and touched my mouth; and the Lord said to me, 'Now, I have put my words in your mouth. See, today I appoint you over nations and over kingdoms, to pluck up and to pull down, to destroy and to overthrow, to build and to plant.' ... [I said], 'Your words were found, and I ate them, and your words became to me a joy and the delight of my heart.' (Jer 1:9-10; 15:16)

Dear friends:

The pain that we experience on the death of a loved one is felt by family members and close friends. With regard to Teresa, I stand outside that circle. I cannot speak of the personal or family life of Teresa because I know little of either. Her own family will pay their tributes to her at the end of this Mass.

They will speak of her as wife, mother, grandmother, sharer of their childhood secrets and teenage hopes, and they will tell of her love and of the blessing she has been in their lives. Teresa knew that I am neither family nor close friend, so what did she want me to say to you in asking that I give her funeral homily? I am not certain. I rummaged around in my mind when I heard she had chosen me and I thought of a time she waited after class to speak with me.

'What was that line again you said about wearing the word of God like a well-tailored suit on a man or an Arnotts outfit on a woman?' she asked me. I had been telling our Bible study class that all of us should aim at becoming so familiar with the word of God, and so in love with it, that it fits us like a well-tailored suit or an Arnotts outfit and we clothe ourselves in ministry with it. And I mentioned a saint – Philip Neri – who is supposed to have said to his students, 'Remember, you may be the only copy of the gospels some people will ever read.' This is a saying that has held true for years in faraway 'pagan' mission fields and may hold true again in years to come in the new mission field of 'post-Christian' Ireland. Christians cannot preach with their lips what is not also seen in their lives.

What linked us, Teresa and me, was our study of the word of God. She was a very quiet member of our Bible study group. We met here every Wednesday morning after the 10 am Mass. And if for some reason she chanced to miss the morning session, she was sure to be present at the evening one after the 7:30 pm Mass.

She came to this deeper and systematic study of the word of God late in her life. But that wasn't her fault. She was just waiting for someone to come to this big and busy parish who had the time to commit to an extended Bible study programme. I was privileged to be that someone, and I was blessed to find seekers of the calibre of Teresa here, people in love with the word of God and longing to probe more deeply its levels of meaning and its layers of love.

The reading from Jeremiah, our second reading at Mass today, was a favourite of Teresa. It was a favourite, I think, because it spoke of her own history, of her hunger for the word of God, and of the way she devoured it with joy when she came upon it, and of how greatly it delighted her heart and lit up her life. She loved to say that the great and gentle St Francis refused to draw-up a special Rule for his religious order, as the founders of other religious orders do, but said instead to his followers, 'My brothers, the gospel is our life and our Rule.'

All who knew her said that she grew with the word of God until she herself became a living, walking word of God among them. Can any greater tribute be paid to a Christian than to say of him or her that this line of scripture, spoken of the Son of God, may be applied in its own way to them too: 'The word became flesh and dwelt among us.' (Jn 1:14)? The scriptural word of God became flesh in Teresa as deeply as any one of us can hope it may become in ourselves. I say that confidently of Teresa. She, in her humility, would never say such a thing of herself. Whatever it is she wanted me to say to you was not something about herself.

I suspect it has to do with the word of God, and I think it has to do with all of you, her friends, as well. And I think it has to do with you, her beloved family, and especially the grandchildren. I think it has to do with our Irish future and with the declining religious milieu in which we will henceforth live – and in which we may live for a long time to come. I think it has to do with wavering faith and the need to be able to fall back on the word of God and rely on it as our comfort, shield and rock in the bad times as in the good. I think it has to do with what she herself found, with what the word of God did to her, and with what God intends it should do for all of us – that, through our study and his grace, we become living, walking, easily read versions of his gospel.

We read in the prophet Isaiah: 'Thus says the Lord, "As the rain and the snow come down from heaven, and return not there but water the earth, making it bring forth and sprout, giving seed to the sower and bread to the eater, so shall my word be that goes forth from my mouth; it shall not return to me empty, but it shall accomplish that which I purpose, and prosper in the thing for which I sent it".' (Is 55: 10-11) The word of God was sent to Teresa to accomplish God's purpose. It shaped her life and she became an inspiration that served and enhanced your life and mine and the life of our parish.

May she rest in peace now in the God who sent her as a word to accomplish his purpose, the same God to whom she has returned, far from empty-handed.

Readings: Wis 3:1-5; Rom 8:14-23; Jn 6:37-40

Angela
(who lived in the shadow of the cross)

The souls of the righteous are in the hand of God, and no torment will ever touch them. In the eyes of the foolish they seemed to have died, and their departure was thought to be a disaster and their going forth from us to be their destruction; but they are at peace. For though in the sight of others they were punished, their hope is full of immortality. Having been disciplined a little, they will receive great good, because God tested them and found them worthy of himself. (Wis 3: 1-5)

Dear friends:

The lives of the Angelas of this world are a challenge to our faith. For they make us face the issue of suffering and the providence of God.

What should I say of my cousin, Angela, and her life? She lived, first as a child who was everyone's dote, next as a beautiful and gifted woman with the world falling at her feet, then as a loving wife and mother, and finally (and for what turned out to be most of her adult life) as a woman of suffering. It would have been merciful if her time had been shortened, but God's will for her was otherwise and we, her family, did not question it.

All of us who have gathered here in support of Michael, Oonagh, Emer and Peter know of the length of Angela's suffering. Only her husband, her children, her close friends, some neighbours, her priests, her doctors and carers know about the depth of it. She had been ill so long she outlasted some of her doctors. At the end of this liturgy, someone will thank them all, and rightly so.

But I must mention here one person uniquely, and that is her marvellous husband, Michael. His devotion and love and care of my cousin were as constant as the sun and the moon, detailed to a fault, outstanding by any standard, even heroic. We thought, at times, that his devotion would kill him, but his faith and God's grace were equal to his need. The challenging part of the marriage vows, 'for better or for worse, for richer or for poorer, in sickness and in health,' was a lived reality in the life of dear Michael.

In one way, Angela was a poor candidate for long-term suffering. Of all her sisters and brothers she was the most outgoing, the most in love with life, the most socially vibrant, the most stylish and fashionable in her young years, the most fun to be with, the most travelled. This made her decline all the more visible, and all the more difficult for her family to watch. And then there was the sheer length of it: the slow stripping away of one thing after another until she was only the shadow of what she had once been. 'My harness piece by piece/ Thou hast hewn from me.' (Francis Thompson, *The Hound of Heaven*) Short-term pain, however intense, is one thing: year after year of piecemeal dismantling is another. But such turned out to be Angela's life.

How did she take it? Poorly and well. Poorly in the sense that she was stubborn as well as intelligent. Sometimes, being stubborn, she would not do what her family wanted for her and sometimes, being intelligent, she consulted her medical encyclopaedias and her MIMS books to question her doctors' advice and check their prescriptions and, let it be said, she was known to change things on occasion.

On the other hand, she took to her dismantling well in the sense that she eventually made the adjustments and met the requirements. In some aspects of her illness she surprised everyone. For example, she went through her cancer surgery and chemo and subsequent checks as if cancer were the least of her concerns. She was not unaware or in denial of it at all: the simple truth is that she had other illnesses to distract her and all that time her only concern was a peculiar pain in her leg and the fact that no one could find out what was causing it. No one ever did.

Angela had a long time to think about suffering because she lived so long with it. I do not know if she thought about it in terms of the great mystery that it is and that she tried to fathom the mystery. All I can say is she met the mystery not in theory but in the flesh, in her flesh, and she learned to live with it through her faith and the care and compassion of others. In this she was like Our Saviour. He never quite explained the mystery either, but tried instead to relieve suffering when he found it in others, and finally took it upon himself and went to the tomb under its weight.

If suffering needs faith to carry it so does the loss of a loved one need faith to transform it. 'Faith is our chance to make sense of loss,' writes American Rabbi David Wolpe in *Making Loss Matter*. We need to make sense of loss when someone we love suffers for years and then is gone and all the suffering seems to have made no sense. Nothing in the world of matter or science can make sense of Angela's life and our loss. But our faith can.

Dr Kathleen Dowling Singh, a specialist in hospice care, says that 'the deepest reason we are afraid of death is that we do not know who we are.' *(The Grace In Dying)* We do not know who we are because we spend our lives trying to be someone or something we are not called to be. We do not know who we are because we do not accept our finiteness, and the truth that our death is a part of our lives. We do not know who we are when we live as escapists from reality and hide behind masks and excuses. We do not know who we are when we insist that God be someone who must keep pain and suffering and death distant from us. Christ has given us our true meaning and identity. He tells us who we are. He makes meaning of our loss, and tells us how pain may be transformed and we through it, and death the passage to another plane.

We are a family committed to Christ. We believe that life has little meaning without him, that we go nowhere without him, but that we will go where he has gone because of our faith and love. We believe with the words of the first reading that the souls of the just are in the hand of God and that no torment shall touch them. We believe that Angela is among the just. We believe that God tried her, as he tries all the just, and found her worthy of himself. We believe that she and we will meet again in the resurrection on the last day. We believe it not because we are great but because our God, in Christ, is so good.

Jesus said to those who love and trust him, and therefore to Angela, and to each one of you here, and to Michael and Oonagh and Emer and Peter, 'Do not let your hearts be troubled. Believe in God, believe also in me. In my Father's house are many dwelling places. If it were not so, would I have told you that I go to prepare a place for you? And if I go and prepare a place for you, I will come again and will take you to myself, that where I am, there you may be also.' (Jn 14: 1-3)

We will meet again in Christ. We will meet again in God's place where there is no more pain and there are no more tears. We will meet again where life and love and joy and bliss are endless, where Angela's yesteryears of suffering, and our loss of today, are transformed by resurrection and enveloped in glory.

Don
(who wasn't sure of the next stage)

[Jesus said], 'When the Son of Man comes in his glory, and all the angels with him, then he will sit on the throne of his glory. All the nations will be gathered before him, and he will separate the people one from another as a shepherd separates the sheep from the goats, and he will put the sheep at his right hand and the goats at the left. Then the king will say to those at his right hand, "Come, you that are blessed by my Father, inherit the kingdom prepared for you from the foundation of the world; for I was hungry and you gave me food, I was thirsty and you gave me drink, I was a stranger and you welcomed me, I was naked and you gave me clothing, I was sick and you took care of me, I was in prison and you visited me." Then the righteous will ask him, "Lord, when was it that we saw you hungry and gave you food, or thirsty and gave you something to drink? And when was it that we saw you a stranger and welcomed you, or naked and gave you clothing? Or when was it that we saw you sick or in prison and visited you?" And the king will answer them, "Truly I tell you, just as you did it to one of the least of these who are members of my family, you did it to me".' (Mt 25:31-40)

Dear friends:

Don has left us after a long and fruitful life. He didn't want a homily and he didn't want a eulogy. Don was emphatic about these things, as he was about much else in life, so the family and I agreed to meet him – half-way! He has the right to his last wishes of course, but we have family rights of remembrance and of celebration too. We know that Don knew he wouldn't have everything his own way on his funeral day.

Not having things his own way was the story of his life. He was honoured as a skilled negotiator, and he was adept in the art of compromise. He also knew he would be a minority of one in the matter of the conduct of his funeral. Maybe that is why he

71

didn't want a homily or a eulogy but suspected there just might be one or the other.

Don was a family man but, like the men of his generation, he was not of the touching type. Behind the flashing intellect and the school principal's detached air was the old-fashioned Irish family man, saying little, touching less, loving much. He was a loving husband, father, and grandfather. His roots were in his family. Don, the public man, retreated to those roots every day after school or meeting to renew himself. Family is the place where we become human, stay grounded in our humanity, and are saved from having to live life on the edge or in the shadows.

Don had a strong sense of logic, of reasoning, and of efficiency. It influenced his children as it influenced himself. Things must be done properly, and if they weren't he wasn't shy in pointing it out 'just for your information, of course'. And he wouldn't point it out if he were not sure 'or at least 99.9% sure'.

Don grew up in Harold's Cross and went to school in Synge Street. He later became vice-principal there. For many years he served on the standing committee of ASTI and served two terms as president. He had the reputation of a formidable and respected negotiator. If he were still in his prime he would, no doubt, have already convinced the government that the teachers' present claims on pay, substitution and supervision are valid, or 'at least 99.9% valid'. His beloved Eileen predeceased him.

In retirement, he lived a quiet, reflective life. His home was his castle. He read, watched television (arguing through the screen with its political guests, especially Albert R. some years back), and tended his garden. He continued to take a great interest in current affairs, the changing scene, all sports, and the progress of his former students. Latterly, his pride was in his fourteen grandchildren and his concern centred more and more on the problems and challenges facing young people. This was Don, always the concerned parent and teacher, with children and students as the pivots of his concern.

His sense of logic and his reasoning roamed through his religious life too. He did not accept – at least not 99.9% – the usual ideas about God, the church, and the afterlife. He saw through the sentimental side of religion, the soft answers and the lived contradictions. He would not settle for what Socrates called 'the unexamined life' (cf Plato, *Apology*), and we respect his theological rigour and his honesty even if a cleric or two didn't during the course of his teaching life. There were times, in the days of the cosy relationship between church and state, when he paid some price for his intellectual rigour and his moral honesty. In religion, as in personal character and work, he was 'straight as an arrow'.

If there are two attributes which best define the God revealed to us by the Old and New Testaments, these attributes are truth and love. 'God is a God of truth,' says Deuteronomy (32:4) in the Old Testament, and Proverbs says of the good man, 'My mouth will utter truth.' (8:7) And 'God is love,' says John (1 Jn 4:16) in the New Testament, and Paul says, 'Owe no one anything, except to love one another; for he who loves his neighbour has fulfilled the law.' (Rom 13:8) No one can fault Don in his quest for truth nor in his active love of his family and students. Perhaps, precisely because these were attributes of Don, as they are of God, he was closer to the Lord than we of the supposedly more orthodox mind and set manner and copper-fastened dogma. In regard to Don, I think the line of Tennyson was valid: 'There lives more faith in honest doubt,/ Believe me, than in half the creeds.' *(In Memoriam)*

It may be, then, for our own comfort as much as for Don's need that we will conclude with some simple lines from one of Fr Frederick Faber's old hymns. If Don needs these lines, let them be our prayer for him. If we need them more than he does, let them be a comfort to us:

There's a wideness in God's mercy,
Like the wideness of the sea;
There's a kindness in his justice
Which is more than liberty.

For the love of God is broader
Than the measures of man's mind;

And the heart of the Eternal
Is most wonderfully kind.

William Barclay calls this 'the infinite sweep of the love of God' and he reckons it to be a fine summing-up of the entire gospel of St Luke. *(The Daily Study Bible: Luke)*

Don, on the other side now, has met this God of the wide mercy, and you and I are here at this Mass for Don doing our best to stretch the mercy even wider because of what is possible in and through Christ. Rest assured that there is room in the width of God's mercy for all the Dons of this world, including our own very special one. And so, we let go of our Dad and our Granddad. We commend him and ourselves to the loving kindness of our God. May we be comforted, and may he rest in peace.

Readings: Lam 3:17-26; Rev 14:13; Lk 15:3-6, 8-9

Jarlath
(who found what he lost)

Jesus told them this parable: 'What one of you, having a hundred sheep and losing one of them, does not leave the ninety-nine in the wilderness, and go after the one which is lost until he finds it? And when he has found it, he lays it on his shoulders, rejoicing. And when he comes home, he calls together his friends and his neighbours, saying to them, "Rejoice with me, for I have found my sheep that was lost ..." Or what woman, having ten silver coins, if she loses one of them, does not light a lamp, sweep the house, and search carefully until she finds it? When she has found it, she calls together her friends and neighbours, saying, "Rejoice with me, for I have found the coin which I had lost".' (Lk 15:3-6, 8-9)

Dear friends:

Cathy and the family agreed that Jarlath would not object to the gospel which we chose for his liturgy, and which we have just listened to. Nor would he object to what we may say of him in terms of that gospel and its tender lessons about the lost and the found. He himself said much to many about his alcoholism and his depression and his years on the streets of Liverpool. He didn't hide his history from anyone, and least of all from the young people for whom he had much concern in his last years.

The gospel parable tells of the sheep which went astray and the coin which was lost. The sheep and the coin speak to us of Jarlath and of the years when he himself was lost. They speak to that grey patch in the middle of his life when depression and alcoholism led him from the home that he and Cathy built, and led him from the hearts which never stopped loving him and holding him up in prayer before the Lord.

One of Shakespeare's plays has the title, *All's Well That Ends Well*. Shakespeare's words console us because I suppose all of us, at one time or another, go through a grey patch which we would prefer to have avoided. The grey patch stands for the time of confusion, or the time of addiction, or the period of squandered opportunity, or the lost years: the period in our histories with little grace or profit in it.

The grey patch may also stand for the illness or the depression that came upon us, and which we never sought, and felt hard done by in its testing. 'In a real dark night of the soul,' wrote F. Scott Fitzgerald, 'it is always three o'clock in the morning, day after day.' *(The Crack-up)* That is one reason why we should be reserved in our judgement of others, and grateful for goodness in our own lives. We never know what patch we might enter at any time, or how we might conduct ourselves in it. In fact, the scripture says we shouldn't judge others at all, because we will most likely misjudge them, and that but for God's grace we go where those we criticise have gone.

What I like about the gospel of the lost sheep and the lost coin is the picture it paints of God. If you and I were the shepherd in the gospel parable, we might leave the single stray sheep to its own devices rather than risk abandoning the ninety-nine obedient sheep. And if you and I were the woman of the house we might be happy enough with our nine safe coins and not turn the house upside down for the sake of the lost one, which we could replace easily anyway.

In fact, you and I would probably do a quick calculation and decide that one sheep and one coin are not worth the effort. And if we lived in the time of the gospel and in the Middle East, we would know that one sheep and one coin were worth very little at all and could easily be replaced in the place where sheep and silver were common enough commodities.

But we are not God and God, thank God, is not us. God does not do calculations. He doesn't operate out of his head, but from his heart. God is the shepherd in the parable and he is the woman in the parable, and Jarlath was – and any one of us could be – the lost sheep and the lost coin. God searches until he finds his lost sheep and he does not quit until he finds the lost coin that is precious to him. The single solitary sheep is precious to the shepherd because he is the model or ideal shepherd, and the single coin is precious because it belongs with the other nine that make up the woman's headband. What was so special about the woman's headband? It was the proud sign of her marriage, the equivalent of the wedding ring in our day. Says William Barclay, in his commentary on Luke's gospel, 'For years maybe, a girl would scrape and save to amass her ten coins.'

Barclay says we should not understand the word 'lost' as eternally lost, but lost in the sense of not being in the place we should be. The place we properly should be is at God's side. When we are not at his side we are lost, and that is heartbreak to him until he finds us.

Jarlath was not where he should have been for quite a while. He was not by God's side. And he was not by Cathy's side and the children's side. He was lost, and then he was found. In his finding, Cathy found again the husband she had lost, and the children their father. And Jarlath found sobriety and lost the worst depths of his depression. And God found again what was his, what he always intended should walk through life at his side as a sheep with his shepherd and as the precious coin on his forehead before his eyes.

In Jarlath's name, I want to do what I know Jarlath himself did many times in his later years: I want to thank Cathy. I want to thank the children and the grandchildren. I want to thank them for keeping faith, for continuing to hope, and for holding Jarlath up in love and prayer through the years when no one knew where he was or how he was, the years that must have been as grey for them as they were for him.

And, in Jarlath's name, I thank the good and gracious Lord who showed himself to be the searching shepherd for Jarlath and, indeed, for the family as well, the Lord who continues to be the searching shepherd for all who place their trust and their confidence in him. I thank him and praise him for being the woman of the house who would not give up her search until she found her precious coin and put it back in its proper place before her eyes. May Jarlath be before God's loving face now, and safely there for ever more.

Readings: Wis 3:1-9; Rev 21:1-4; Mt 25:31-40

Eileen
(who was Granny to everyone)

I saw a new heaven and a new earth; for the first heaven and the first earth had passed away, and the sea was no more. And I saw the holy city, new Jerusalem, coming down out of heaven from God, prepared as a bride adorned for her husband. And I heard a loud voice from the throne saying, 'See, the home of God is among mortals. He will dwell with them as their God; they will be his peoples, and God himself will be with them; he will wipe every tear from their eyes. Death will be no more; mourning and crying and pain will be no more, for the first things have passed away.' And the one who was seated on the throne said, 'See, I am making all things new.' (Rev 21:1-4)

Dear friends:

When someone we love leaves us there is a big empty space in our lives. Things are never quite the same again. So we look, first of all, for assurance that Eileen is in a good place, and we look for comfort for ourselves. Jesus said, 'I am the resurrection and the life; [she] who believes in me, though [she] die, yet shall [she] live.' (Jn 11: 25) If anyone ever believed in Jesus, and followed him lovingly, it was our Eileen.

For all of us, her family and friends, we have the comfort of our faith and the comfort of our memories. For Dan, her spouse, some memories are, of course, special and unique to him. He alone can cherish them and he alone will be cherished in them.

For the children and grandchildren, there are great memories that will never leave them, memories of a mother and a Granny of faith and love and endless concern. She was an angel who fluttered about them, always planning and plotting on their behalf, a sometimes stubborn angel it's true, but always an angel intent on their best interests. You have great memories that will support and warm you in the sometimes lonely days ahead.

Love is the primary Christian value and it has to express itself in concrete actions, not just in nice sentiments. Those we know best are the people we live with. It is surely, then, a testament to Eileen's love that Dan should define her as a woman who was always thinking of others and always doing for them. But we knew this ourselves from our long personal experience of her goodness.

At first glance, an outsider might see Granny as just a 'half-citified' country woman, but a country woman at heart if one were to judge her by her simple attire or her hairpinned head. Few would see her as a contemporary woman. But appearances are deceiving. She was the first woman from her parish to attend university and most of her adult life was spent in the halls of academia. She combined a university career with marriage and child-rearing in the years when it was unusual here. Unusual too for her time was her sense of democracy and equality. She made no distinction between colleague and floor cleaner in the early days of Belfield – nor between Irish and English and native and foreigner. Her friends were from all walks of life and more than one or two from no discernible walk of life at all.

Her interests included a noteworthy stamp collection, cine movies, auctions and sales of work. She was not 'into' the high-calibre stuff and would gladly call herself just a bargain hunter. She loved bargains. All kinds of them. She loved stuff. All kinds of it. She unloaded all of these bargains, all this stuff turned into treasure by her love, on her family whether they wanted it or not!

Curracloe was her adopted home and, in a way, her heart. She bought it – long before Irish holiday homes were *au courant* – as a getaway place for the family and a meeting place for friends. It was the holy ground for family gatherings and celebrations of all kinds. Now it is a place of memories, and a loving legacy to her children and grandchildren. May it continue to be so, off into the future, generation after generation. She would expect that of you, and want that for you. Down in Curracloe, especially, she was known as Granny. She was Granny not just to her own grandchildren but to everybody down there and to their children and grandchildren. She took a quiet delight in this omnipotence.

The car was central to Granny's life. How she loved it for what it did for her! It was the life-long badge of the modern side of her and, above all, it was a tool of her independence. It got her where she wanted to go, when she wanted to go. It would normally be loaded with children or friends when it wasn't loaded with bargains and stuff and 'treasures' of all kinds for you. Cathy remarked that when Eileen arrives at heaven's gate her first words to Peter will be, 'Where do I apply for a driving licence?'

As she got older, some of us wondered how she might leave this life. Would it be at home in Dublin, or by the sea in Curracloe, or would it be that scourge of modern life, cancer, calling late for her? I suppose, deep down, we were thinking of her age, and of her new inclination to tire easily, and of that car of hers rushing on its latest bargain hunt or racing back loaded with more stuff for us. How shocked we were when it proved to be none of these but a quick decline after a rather minor accident!

We will not dwell here on our shock or her pain. We will only thank God that it was short, and we will thank him publicly for her wonderful carers. And we will say a prayer for ourselves and our future in which, I think, we see the reflection of our dearest Granny especially in her most recent past:

When the signs of age begin to mark my body
(and still more when they touch my mind);
when the ill that is to diminish me or carry me off
strikes from without or is born in me;
when the painful moment comes
in which I suddenly awaken
to the fact that I am ill or growing old;
and above all at that last moment
when I feel I am losing hold of myself
and am absolutely passive within the hands
of the great unknown forces that have formed me;

in all those dark moments, O God,
grant that I may understand that it is you
(provided only my faith is strong enough)
who are painfully parting the fibres of my being
in order to penetrate to the very marrow
of my substance and bear me away within yourself.
(Teilhard de Chardin)

May God take our dear Granny to himself, and may he comfort
all of us.

Readings: *Lam 3:17-26; 1 Jn 3:1-2; Mt 19:13-15*

Margaret
(who went back to the beginning)

Then little children were being brought to him in order that he might lay his hands on them and pray. The disciples spoke sternly to those who brought them; but Jesus said, 'Let the little children come to me, and do not stop them; for it is to such as these that the kingdom of heaven belongs.' And he laid his hands on them. (Mt 19:13-15)

Dear friends:

When you outlive almost everybody you once knew there are likely to be few people around for your funeral. The case is doubly so when you've spent many years in a nursing home, hidden in a quiet corner of a large city parish and far from the Connemara of your childhood. Such is Margaret's case. We scheduled her funeral Mass for this time of our usual 10 am Mass so that she would not be alone, and you would be here, and I would introduce her to you, and you and I together would sent her home to God.

Who was Margaret? No relatives were found, for us to inform them of her death or they to tell us about her. The nursing home knows little about her and the solicitor, who managed her affairs, knows only a slight bit more. She was born in England before the First World War. Her parents moved back to Connemara and she grew up there. They lived on a small farm. They returned to England after the war, and at some stage Margaret lost her parents. We know nothing of the circumstances. She worked as a domestic most of her life, never married, seems to have kept to herself, and she had a small British pension.

She was gentle, harmless, unobtrusive, asking for nothing, no bother at all to anyone. She lived greatly in her own world, and a stranger might think that she was out of touch with reality. But she wasn't. She found enough in her own head to sustain a balanced life right to the end. Perhaps her head carried mostly good memories, or perhaps it was that her heart had long since forgotten old hurts.

She was out and about most days, a measure of her sanity and of her health. But you'd hardly notice her small frail figure except when the wind blew in off the bay and made a sail of herself and her raincoat, and you saw her holding on to a door knob or the corner of a wall so she wouldn't blow back down Lower Salthill.

Actually, she was here in this church often for a visit, and when she was younger and stronger she visited the Lord daily in the Jes. and the Claddagh as well. I know that some of you were aware of her, with the plastic blue rosary beads around her neck, and that whenever you smiled at her you got a child's smile back, but never a word in return for your word. I suspect the reason for this was that she lost her English and remembered only her childhood language. Towards the end she spoke little at all and then only *as Gaeilge.* Was it a sign that her life was drawing to a close?

When Pat our custodian heard of her passing he said simply, 'Ah, the poor creature!' He meant it in the way we Irish mean it; as a mark of special concern and affection. I wish I could tell you more about her and offer a litany of light and love in her favour, but I can't. She is one of those aged and kithless souls in our cities who are no longer really known to anyone but God. Let us send her home to him through Our Lady, and in her own language, and with the prayer she kept pinned to the tablecloth by her bed in the nursing home:

A Mhuire Bheannaithe,
Bí trócaireach liom,
labhair le Dia ar mo shon.
Inis dó gur créatúr bocht mé
lán de pheacaí ó bharr go bun,
ach gráim thú, a Mháthair dhílis,
ortsa i dtólamh a bhíos mo ghrá.
Déan impí ormsa le Cruthaitheoir Nimhe,
agus beidh mé buíoch díot go brách. Amen.

DEATH OF AN OLD PERSON

Readings: Wis 3:1-9; Rom 8:31-35, 37-39; Jn 12:23-28

Fergus
(who lived a long life)

Jesus said, 'The hour has come for the Son of Man to be glorified. Very truly, I tell you, unless a grain of wheat falls into the earth and dies, it remains just a single grain; but if it dies, it bears much fruit. Those who love their life lose it, and those who hate their life in this world will keep it for eternal life. Whoever serves me must follow me, and where I am, there will my servant be also. Whoever serves me, the Father will honour.

Now is my soul troubled. And what should I say – "Father, save me from this hour"? It is for this reason that I have come to this hour. Father, glorify your name.' Then a voice came from heaven, 'I have glorified it, and I will glorify it again.' (Jn 12:23-28)

Dear friends:

Fergus was only four years short of the President's cheque. It would have raised plumes of pride on his white head if the Lord had given him the four years; and if a *Fianna Fáil*-er were the President at the time of the presentation, so much the better! But such was not to be.

However, Fergus was an old-timer, with the old time courtesies and the old-time faith, and he said his prayers and counted his blessings every day. He was a man grateful for the small as well as the big graces. He would never insist of God that he should be given those four years just to complete a century, as if God were the scorekeeper at a cricket match. Fergus never questioned the mind of 'the Man above'. Besides, I imagine he was sufficiently happy with the fact that the party of his choice are in power in this the time of his passing! And the Lord, I'm sure, knows well that this is the reason for the special smile he sees on Fergus' soul.

When people live to a big age they are asked the secret of

their long life. They usually say things like, 'I never smoked and I never drank' or 'I took regular exercise and went to bed early' or 'I kept away from frys and fats'. Well, Fergus loved a fry in the morning and a Jameson or two before going to bed fairly late at night, and he also loved going to Knock to honour Our Lady whenever he could get a lift. Now that, surely, is an unusual combination of things, an odd recipe for health and longevity, and I don't know what the experts would make of it!

Fergus lived long enough to be known and loved by multitudes, and the range of ages and tastes and political persuasions in the pews here this morning, and at the funeral home and here in church last night, is the measure of that widespread respect and love for Fergus. As he grew older, and as the generations increased, he was known in the city simply as Fergus, and there are some here who never ever knew his last name until it was announced on Galway Bay FM with the funeral arrangements.

Fergus remembered such events as the loss of the *Titanic* in 1912 and the *Lusitania* in 1917, 'the guns of August' in 1914, the Easter Rising in 1916, a family visit by Liam Mellowes, and the three months of his father's internment in Frongoch prison camp in Wales. As he grew older he became a sort of icon to all who knew of these things only from their school history books or a PC search engine.

Fergus lost his dear Anne many years ago. He cared for her as she declined with what the late Canon Heaney called 'the dedication of a guardian angel'. He had no children to support him in his care of Anne. Those were times when the country was poor and special care services for the sick were the luxury of the rich. It is a mark of the Christian spirit of the people of that time that Fergus' and Anne's neighbours were angels of mercy. May I pay public tribute here to those of them who are still with us and to those others who have gone home to their reward.

Few of us know, perhaps, that Fergus was an electrician by trade and that he was very much involved in the electrification of this city and county after 1929. Few of us know, perhaps, that he worked in Manhattan at the time of the Wall Street crash, that he intended to spend his life in America, but, like many of his generation, was called home to care for his parents as TB afflicted them in the time it was known most fearfully as consumption. Perhaps it was this caring life of his, taken up so much by the unexpected need of others, that made him so pragmatically Christian and so accessible and loved by all of us his friends.

We mourn his passing only because of his goodness and because the world is always so much less a place for the loss of such truly human beings and old-time gentlemen as Fergus. On the other hand, we let him go after a long and fruitful life. We let him go in acceptance of God's will, and because we know the place where he is going, and because he deserves the best that only God can give, and can give only where the Ferguses and the Annes of the world are overwhelmed with love at his side in the everlasting bliss of heaven.

May his truly noble and Christian soul rest now in peace.

Readings: *Dan 12:1-3; Rom 8:31-35, 37-39; Jn 14:1-6*

Eleanor
(who was a friend of God and a prophet)

[Daniel said], 'At that time Michael, the great prince, the protector of your people, shall arise. There shall be a time of anguish, such as has never occurred since nations first came into existence. But at that time your people shall be delivered, everyone who is found written in the book. Many of those who sleep in the dust of the earth shall awake, some to everlasting life, and some to shame and everlasting contempt. Those who are wise shall shine like the brightness of the sky, and those who lead many to righteousness, like the stars forever and ever.' (Dan 12:1-3)

Dear friends:

We gather for our final farewell to dear Eleanor. The church discourages us from turning the funeral homily into a eulogy, i.e. into a hymn of praise for the departed one. In Eleanor's case I do not have the spiritual depth to be able to craft a eulogy which might even begin to describe this remarkable woman and do justice to her spiritual depth and wisdom. I can only allude to some of Eleanor's Christian character and qualities.

What a sheer blessing she has been to us, and what a grace it has been just to know her!

We offer our condolences to Brian, her cousin, and our gratitude to the staff of St Alban's nursing home who tended her so professionally and so devotedly. They, too, feel her loss for she was equally a grace and a blessing for them as for ourselves. Perhaps nursing staff cannot always say that of their patients.

I suppose every parish priest looks at his parish now and then hoping to see the evidence of sanctity in it. Perhaps he is looking mostly for reassurance with regard to the value of his ministry and the value of all the homilies and talks and novenas and parish missions that take place during his tenure. If he looks to someone like Eleanor, he will not find that reassurance. The fact is that she wasn't here for any of the homilies, talks, novenas and parish missions. She was in the nursing home. But sanctity she had. She developed it somewhere other than the parish.

I wasn't all that long in this parish when one of the priests alerted me to the holiness and the wisdom of Eleanor by saying, 'I'm a bit down at the minute. I'm going over to the nursing home to see Eleanor. She always helps me see things right.' He wasn't off to see the Franciscans or the bishop for some spiritual uplifting, and obviously I didn't fit the bill either. But Eleanor did.

Where did Eleanor get her spiritual wisdom? Where did she get her inner peace which so radiated from her that it calmed you down as soon as you sat in her presence and you could feel it entering you in an almost physical way? She found it in quiet recollection in God's presence. We need to do the same. The Jewish Psalmist told us a long time ago, 'Be still, and know that I am God.' (Ps 46:10) He also said, 'The Lord is my shepherd, I shall not want; he makes me lie down in green pastures. He leads me beside still waters; he restores my soul. He leads me in paths of righteousness.' (Ps 23: 1-2)

Too many of us are too busy these days to live on the inside and from the inside, and to let God shepherd us. We do not allow ourselves time to rest in the green pastures that are the pages of the word of God. We are too busy to draw inspiration from the still waters of recollection and contemplation so as to restore our weary spirits. We are, perhaps, like Martha 'anxious and troubled about many things' but not developing our inner space, the 'one thing needed'. (Lk 10:41-42)

Others are caught up in the rat race on the outside and in their busy-body world on the inside. They seem to believe that nature has given them heads and hearts only for busy-ness: for tasks, projects, schedules and problem-solving. 'In [our] pragmatic society, doing counts for everything, being counts for nothing.' (Ronald Rolheiser, *The Shattered Lantern*) It is an awful spiritual mistake.

Are you and I, too, running ourselves ragged? Are we reinforcing the psychology of our culture which believes that if you aren't always doing something you count for nothing and don't know who you are? Always doing has come to define us. But that is false. Many people don't know who they are because they don't rest long enough to allow God to whisper in their ear and tell them. The inner peace and the bestowing peace of Eleanor, and the holiness of her life are testimony that her way is the genuine way to live, connected with God, receiving peace, bestowing peace, seeing all things in the light of the revealing word and Spirit, and offering the wise word, the spirit-lifting line to anyone with eyes to see and ears to hear.

What I am eulogising here may be considered out-of-touch by the so-called with-it people of our time. But how wrong they are! Eleanor disproves them. And so do their own drooping spirits and shot nerves. When we rest with the Lord in his presence, and think over his directing words, everything recovers its proper stature, has its place, and is seen in its proper light. False values are demoted, and good ones recover what was theirs before over-secularity and the rat race assaulted and robbed them. It is only in the presence of God, dear friends, and through his word and Spirit, and by quiet recollection that people and things, projects and tasks, are restored to their proper places and we ourselves to a balanced life.

The theologian Elizabeth A. Johnson says that in every generation 'the great Spirit of God, Holy Wisdom ... passes into holy souls ... and makes them friends of God and prophets.' (Truly Our Sister: A Theology of Mary in the Communion of Saints) Her words echo the Book of Wisdom which says, 'In every generation wisdom passes into holy souls, she makes them friends of God and prophets ... she is indeed more splendid than the sun.' (Wis 7:27, 29) The Spirit of God and his wisdom passed into Eleanor and made her the friend of God and a soft-spoken, gentle prophet who guided more than one layperson and more than one priest.

May she watch over us now from where we believe her to be, God's place. Daniel quotes the Jewish Book of Predestination in our first Mass reading today, 'Those who are wise shall shine like the brightness of the sky, and those who lead many to righteousness, like the stars for ever and ever.' (Dan 12:3) We may allow ourselves the belief that he was speaking of the Eleanors of his time, and of the Eleanors of all the Christian generations yet to come, and of the particular Eleanor of our knowing, time and grace.

Readings: Is 25:6-9; Acts 10: 34-39; Mt 25:31-40

Mattie
(who left a trail of lights behind him)

Peter began to speak to them, 'I truly understand that God shows no partiality, but in every nation anyone who fears him and does what is right is acceptable to him. You know the message he sent to the people of Israel, preaching peace by Jesus Christ – he is the Lord of all. That message spread throughout Judea, beginning in Galilee after the baptism that John announced: how God anointed Jesus of Nazareth with the Holy Spirit and with power; how he went about doing good and healing all who were oppressed by the devil, for God was with him. We are witnesses to all that he did both in Judea and in Jerusalem.' (Acts 10:34-39)

Dear friends:

I suppose that we, the children of the age of mass media, are used to watching the big funerals on TV of the 'people that count' or reading about them in the papers and glossy magazines. All of these people are wealthy or famous or 'socially significant'. They are eulogised in the press. They are given special notice. Great things are said about them.

Then we come to the 'small people' of the world, such as Mattie. His passing from the stage of life has not made any headlines. There may be a note of his passing in one of the city papers later this week. On the other hand, there may not be. For Mattie left behind no family, nor wealth, nor sports club, nor local branch of a political party. He will remain unsung except by the angels and ourselves and those who were the beneficiaries of his Christian heart.

I think that every Bible scholar I've read says that the job of the Christian is to witness to Christ. Witnessing to Christ is, in fact, the original meaning of the word saint in the early days of the church. And I think that all the scholars say that this witnessing is not a matter of words but of deeds. As the Little Flower once put it: 'The most beautiful thoughts are nothing without good deeds.' *(A Little Book of Thérèse of Lisieux)*

Our second reading at this Mass for Mattie was taken from the Acts of the Apostles. In it we heard a fine definition of Jesus, based on how his contemporaries viewed him. This is what they said of him: 'He went about doing good.' In parallel fashion, St Paul admonishes us, 'Let us not grow weary in doing what is right, for we will reap at harvest time, if we do not give up. So then, whenever we have an opportunity, let us work for the good of all, and especially for those of the family of faith.' (Gal 6:9)

Mattie went through the years of his life, like Jesus, doing good. Nothing spectacular of course, nothing to make the front pages or the glossy magazines, because he wasn't wealthy or famous or had the wherewithal to move mountains or redistribute the national wealth. Nonetheless, he went about doing good. He did things that were socially and spiritually significant in this parish and in this city. He did his good mostly hidden from our eyes, and mostly with the St Vincent de Paul Society – which has done for generations and which continues to do so much good. He did it at the level on which so many people still live lives of 'quiet desperation', as Henry Thoreau put it in *Walden*, lives of quiet desperation even in our still quite prosperous economy.

All the poverty Mattie saw and tried to lessen, all the misery he met and tried to relieve, all the frustration he faced and tried to soothe is known only to God because he was walking our streets doing good before most of us here ever heard of him. And, as you know, he sounded no trumpet before his face but was as silent about his work as a man under an oath of secrecy to the poor he served.

The scholar William Barclay, in his *Daily Study Bible*, tells a story from the life of the essayist and historian, Thomas Carlyle, which I think found its incarnation in our Mattie. One evening, he writes, a guest was visiting Carlyle at his isolated farm in Scotland. Darkness began to descend. The guest expected

Carlyle to light a lamp but the great man didn't. He seemed to be waiting for something to happen.

After a time, Carlyle pointed the guest to where there was a hill on the far side of the valley. The guest couldn't see it in the dark. But, suddenly, a light appeared on the hill, and then another and another and another as though forming a chain. It was the unseen lamplighter moving up the street of the village on the side of the hill and lighting one lamp after another and bringing light where previously there was darkness. 'Every Christian should be as that unseen lamplighter,' said Carlyle. A Christian is one who goes through life quietly banishing the darkness with the light of good deeds.

Mattie was our lamplighter. He went through the years of his life and the night streets of our parish and city like the unseen lamplighter on Carlyle's hill. In imitation of Jesus 'he went about doing good and healing all that were oppressed.' He left a trail of lights behind him. May Jesus now give him his 'share in the inheritance of the saints in light.' (Col 1:12)

Readings: Is 25:6-9; 1 Thess 4:13-18; Lk 4:16-21

Tim
(who ministered to the end)

When [Jesus] came to Nazareth, where he had been brought up, he went to the synagogue on the sabbath day, as was his custom. He stood up to read, and the scroll of the prophet Isaiah was given to him. He unrolled the scroll and found the place where it was written: 'The Spirit of the Lord is upon me, because he has anointed me to bring good news to the poor. He has sent me to proclaim release to captives and recovery of sight to the blind, to let the oppressed go free, to proclaim the year of the Lord's favour.' And he rolled up the scroll, gave it back to the attendant, and sat down. The eyes of all in the synagogue were fixed on him. Then he began to say to them, 'Today this scripture has been fulfilled in your hearing.' (Lk 4:16-21)

Dear friends:

The last time Tim flew out to South Africa, where he had spent all of his healthy years as a priest, he made his confession with the Esker Redemptorists the evening before. Not that a priest of his quality needed confession. He had September the 11th still on his mind, and his age and his indifferent medical history. But mostly, I think, he went to confession because he was of that generation which liked to be doubly sure of its peace with God before undertaking any journey that took them beyond the Shannon!

As a priest, Tim was a mix of the old and the new. He was traditional in his piety and in his public theology, and all his years did not seem to move him very far from those safe old All Hallows anchorages. On the other hand, he asked the deeper questions in private, and was less than awed by any textbook answers. Yet it struck me that, however deep the questions or tenuous the answers, Tim's faith had a child's simplicity to it: it was deeper than all the questions and all the possible answers as well. All the tough questions would have to wait for their last level of illumination in the great and glorious revelation of the last day. And Tim was content to wait.

There was great nature to Tim, as the old people used to say, though a succession of newly minted curates in South Africa might not agree! His great nature made him naturally ecumenical before Vatican II. It made him understanding of the many religions of the world, and of the many forms of faith in Christian history, and of the many shades of Catholic faith one finds today in every parish. The individual's own psychology accounted for this form and shade, angle and slant and nuance.

Tim was not surprised by the twists and turns of the human heart. The heart is something that cannot be copper-fastened by dogma, and Tim well knew it. He said to me one time, 'I know well why scripture says that only God can look into the human heart and judge it properly.' For Tim, the Bible was more than a holy book. It was, like Shakespeare, a library of insight into human psychology and Tim, to my mind, became in his journey through life a small book of the same insight and understanding himself.

He had a way of overlooking human failings and his natural humanity helped him in this. So did his sense of humour. On the other hand, he was capable of calling a parishioner or a curate to account when he thought it necessary or, as the old spiritual writers put it, when he deemed it salutary. He expected a lot from curates in his time but I don't think it was ever as much as he was willing to do himself for the people, and we saw that here at home even in his last years when he would not listen to the medical advice but served and soldiered on as best he could.

The homily at a priest's funeral often lists his so-called pastoral accomplishments. These are usually physical things – the church or the chapel he built and maybe even the school and the shrine he put up and, more recently, the millennium marker he put down. I've never had immense *grá* for this slant on priestly ministry and accomplishment but Tim would not dismiss it. For he was himself of the so-called bricks-and-mortar generation of priests. He saw value in leaving a mark or a scratch on the landscape to show, as he once said, that we too passed this way. At his 40th anniversary of ordination celebration in All Hallows his bricks-and-mortar accomplishments in Africa were listed. They were, in truth, considerable. And we know they would have been even more if poor health hadn't brought him home before his time. I will not repeat them here. Besides, the man and the priest that was Tim cannot be measured only in stones.

I once heard a Connemara man say at a funeral, 'Gems are buried with Seán.' He was referring to Seán's gifts of imagination and his agility with words. Tim was capable of gems too. For example, only a few days ago he said to me, 'Crossing the last bridge, only God can hold my hand.' Today, gems of an even higher order are buried with Tim, and I, as you, greatly mourn the passing of their richness from our lives, from society, and from our church.

Tim's higher order gems were the old virtues, the old decencies if you wish. They were his loyalty to his friends, his trustworthiness, his hospitality, his kindness, his striking care of the sick and the elderly and anyone in distress, his lack of make-believe in pastoral ministry, his plain goodness and humanity. In the age of hype and spin and fudge and cover-up and posturing and affectation, Tim's decencies were gems indeed and they are sorely lost with his passing to present-day society and to present-day church.

I want to offer my deepest sympathy to Tim's family and old friends. I want to thank them, and all who cared for him in the latter years. Perhaps he may not have realised how caring you were of him and how much his health and self-confidence relied on your care. Perhaps he may not have realised how great a part you played in his being able to soldier on in his pursuit of the old All Hallows vision of its missionary priests dying with their boots on and all the straps and buckles of their harness still in their proper fastenings.

For you as for me the news last Thursday, though never entirely unexpected, was yet a shock. For Tim had rallied before

and, I suppose, deep down we thought he might rally again. But
this time it was to be different. Our shock is in the finality of it.
There will be no more of rallying and of return to us. We are left
this time only with our memories. What can we say of last
Thursday but that

The tide ran in, that day, so deep
The sun was drowned; yet friendship flows
Deeper, from springs which childhood knows,
Mirrored in ageing memory.

(Jim Aldous in Lyn Macdonald, *To The Last Man: Spring 1918*)
The tide was too deep for Tim that day. But we will hold him in
the mirror of our memory. We will hold him in our hearts while
we wait for that day promised by the Lord to all who believe, the
day when we and Tim will meet again in a great and certain
future. Let us listen to the comforting words of our friend and
brother-priest, St Paul:

We do not want you to be uninformed, brothers and sisters,
about those who have died, so that you may not grieve as
others do who have no hope. For since we believe that Jesus
died and rose again, even so, through Jesus, God will bring
with him those who have died. For this we declare to you by
the word of the Lord, that we who are alive, who are left until
the coming of the Lord, will by no means precede those who
have died. For the Lord himself, with a cry of command, with
the archangel's call and with the sound of God's trumpet,
will descend from heaven, and the dead in Christ will rise
first. Then we who are alive, who are left, will be caught up
in the clouds together with them to meet the Lord in the air;
and so we will be with the Lord forever. Therefore encourage
one another with these words.' (1 Thess 4:13-18)

DEATH OF A RELIGIOUS SISTER
Readings: Job 19:1, 23-27; Rom 8:31-35, 37-39; Lk 1:46-55

Maura
(faithful through the changing years)

And Mary said, 'My soul magnifies the Lord, and my spirit rejoices in God my Saviour, for he has looked with favour on the lowliness of his servant. Surely, from now on all generations will call me blessed; for the Mighty One has done great things for me, and holy is his name. His mercy is for those who fear him from generation to generation. He has shown strength with his arm, he has scattered the proud in the thoughts of their hearts. He has brought down the powerful from their thrones, and lifted up the lowly; he has filled the hungry with good things, and sent the rich away empty. He has helped his servant Israel, in remembrance of his mercy, according to the promise he made to our ancestors, to Abraham and to his descendants forever.' (Lk 1:46-55)

Dear friends:

In our vigil gathering for Maura last night we heard a resume of her life and an account of her achievements in teaching and in social work in the west of Ireland and in California. Here, at her funeral Mass, I would like to focus on her lifelong fidelity as a Christian and as a religious Sister.

In doing this I am trying to pay tribute to all of you Sisters as well, and especially to you of Maura's generation who lived through a time of great change in the church and in your lives. You were yourselves among the agents of change despite its many upsetting aspects as it uprooted us from our previous Tridentine zone of comfort, or maybe stagnancy. Change in the church was hard on Maura initially and, I think, because it came when she was settled and happy enough in the old way.

I don't think change of itself is a great challenge. Change is of the nature of life and of the living of our lives. As the poet Rilke put it, 'Our life passes in transformation.' *(Duino Elegies)* I think that the average person is well able to adjust to normal change and even able to adjust to fairly radical change at least every now and then. Real change for me is what happens to people in such calamities as the uprooting and destruction of the great famines and wars of history. I'm always in awe of famine victims and war refugees. They are the ones who know what real change is. By way of contrast, the changes of Vatican II were hardly anything at all. However, the kind of unending, slow-drip, often hit-and-miss change that has marked our lifetime in church and in vocation has been a bridge too far for many of our companions. It is not my brief to judge them but to understand and accept their difficulties.

Maura felt the stress of change in her middle years as a Sister just when she thought she was settled for life. More so, she felt the stress of the kind of change that, she believed, did not know where it was going or if it would ever stop. So she went off to your high school in California – for relief! She found things farther ahead there, but not always to her liking. For one thing, there was a new and unexpected challenge for her called 'American speed,' and there were those American liturgical experiments that came and went like the lunar tides.

When she came back she found things changing too slowly here, or hardly at all, and sometimes, she felt, in reverse. For example, as the tabernacle of the Lord's presence was being moved away from 'the table of the altar' the portrait of the Pope or Our Lady of Medjudjore was being placed in front of it. That one caused her real grief! But instead of dropping out she did the wise thing: she took the changes that were happening and the changes that were not happening and made it all grist for a deeper personal spiritual life.

Church change, its speed or petty pace, its sense and nonsense, became a part of her daily companionship with Christ and of her inner journey to spiritual maturity. This is the fidelity in her regard that I referred to a few moments ago. Hers became not the fidelity of the trapped and embittered spirit, nor the fidelity of the implacable conservative and liberal to an immovable position, nor the fidelity of the stiff upper lip, but that positive fidelity which is the mark of our sharing in the cross of Christ and of our trust in him that all will be well since all is his and he is God's. (see 1 Cor 3:23)

Our gospel today is the Magnificat. We tend to read it sentimentally and in a politely sanitised interpretation. But it is neither sentimental nor polite: it is radical. William Barclay calls it the most revolutionary hymn in history. It is about change, major change, in us and in our world, change set-off by Mary's conception of the Child who will transform the world – and religion too – and turn accepted values upside down. We are drawn, you and I, by our baptism and our vocation into this vortex of change, and as its collaborating agents in our own time and place. For this reason if none other, change should be second nature to us, and we should be the last people in the world to oppose it when it calls for reform, renewal, or even the turning of our lives upside down.

We tend to read the infancy narrative sentimentally or politely as well. But the real birth of Jesus has nothing sentimental or polite about it. It is a hard matter of the night, of a long journey, a strange town, no room, a stable, cold and poverty, animals and dung. It is a matter, too, of what Elizabeth A. Johnson calls 'no relatives ... no midwife and bloodiness.' (*Truly Our Sister: A Theology of Mary in the Communion of Saints*) For Johnson, 'the memory of Mary' (i.e. a truthful history of Mary) is a quite 'dangerous' one. It is dangerous in the sense that it demythologises our usual sweet view of Mary, asks uncomfortable questions of ourselves, of our traditional theologies and pieties, and of present church structures (even after Vatican II), and in the sense that it calls us to experience, as Mary did, poverty, humility, the sword of discernment and the anguish of losing what or who is precious to us.

But such is the nature of the Christian way and the Christian life. Through it all, God calls us to be trusting of him and to be faithful. And all of this poverty and stripping and discerning and losing – and finding – is the hammer and the anvil on which we are forged and tempered and tested and refined as the children of God. Someone has written, 'God does not ask us to be successful, but to be faithful.' How true that is in life! How telling a lesson for ourselves and our changing times! And how well Maura proved it in her own life in the long run!

Through all the changes in life or in church, and more fundamental than any of them, is our call to be faithful to the Christ who is ever faithful to us. We allow nothing to injure that priority, much less to separate us from him. Everything in our lives is grist to the mill for our spiritual growth 'until we attain ... the measure of the stature of the fullness of Christ.' (Eph 4:13)

Ag Críost an síol,
ag Críost an fómhar,
in iothlainn Dé go dtugtar sinn.

Ag Críost an mhuir,
ag Críost an t-iasc,
i líonta Dé go gcastar sinn.

Ó fhás go haois
is ó aois go bás
do dhá láimh, a Chríost, anall tharainn.

Ó bhás go críoch
nach críoch ach athfhás,
i bParthas na ngrás go rabhaimid.
(Ár bPaidreacha Dúchais)

Readings: Jer 31:15-16; 1 Cor 2:7-9; Mk 10:13-16

Niamh
(who left us so soon)

A voice is heard in Ramah, lamentation and bitter weeping. Rachel is weeping for her children; she refuses to be comforted ... because they are no more ... 'Keep your voice from weeping, and your eyes from tears; for there is a reward for your work,' says the Lord, 'and they shall come back from the land of the enemy.' (Jer 31:15-16)

Dear friends:

The greatest blessing God gives Noreen and Jim in this time of loss is their faith. The second blessing God gives them is their youthfulness and a future still full of years and the promise of fruitfulness. The third blessing is the immense outpouring of love and support for Noreen and Jim from their families, neighbours, friends and this their parish community.

Niamh hadn't made it even halfway to her first birthday when God called her back to himself. Her few months were a tremendous stress on Noreen and Jim, and a huge struggle for life on the part of tiny Niamh. The odds were always against her, even in this day of advanced technology and the medical miracle. Perhaps that's the reason God called her back to himself. There was nothing medicine could do for her here.

I have no easy theology to cover the death of an infant. I have no easy theology to explain why death came upon you so soon, tiny Niamh. Your very littleness and fragility increases my difficulty. I could pull straws from a questionable theological wind and say things like 'God wanted another little angel in heaven so he chose you.' But such a line is a two-edged sword, and the poet Wordsworth is whispering in my ear that he is not happy with it:

A simple child,
That lightly draws its breath

And feels its life in every limb:
What should it know of death?
(We are Seven)

I could put tiny you into the big theology of original sin and name you an unfortunate consequence of the flawed nature that original sin left us as a terrible legacy. I could tell you that this flawed nature lifts its destroying hand indiscriminately from time to time and, all too often, picks out the least and the most vulnerable among us. But all that is too removed from you and from the anguish of your loving parents, Noreen and Jim. And it is too remote for all of us when such a tiny, innocent life like your own is lost. What does any of it have to do with your darling parents who will have to fight doubt and false guilt as well as grief? What does it have to do with your darling Mum who carried you inside her for nine months, and had dreams for you, and spoke a thousand small words to you before you even saw the light of day, and named a hundred hopes for you, and made up little love songs for you, only to see you struggle in our alien world for four-and-a-half months and lose your battle at the end of it?

Your passing is beyond us, beyond our usual theologies and our explanations. We feel in our bones that you had the right to a fair chance in life and that you didn't get it. We feel that death could have made his choice somewhere else or of someone else ...

If death had need
To pass our town,
Why could he not take
An old woman past her time?

(Pádraig J. Daly, 'A Mháire, A Mhuirnin,' *The Last Dreamers*)

I could tell God that your dear parents and all of us here are able to make easy sense of many deaths but not of yours; that we understand death when it is due to man's wars and violence, or on the completion of the biblical age of 'three score and ten years, or eighty if we are strong' (Ps 90:10); that we understand the death of the long-suffering, and even the death of the ones of short but fruitful years who achieved so much – people such as Jesus who left us at thirty-three, the Little Flower at twenty-four, and Maria Goretti at scarcely fourteen. But you, tiny Niamh, your death puzzles us. You will have to help us understand it and so give acceptance of it to our hearts.

If you could speak, what would you say to us, and especially to Mum and Dad, from where you are now? Would you tell them that you are in heaven; that you are with the very first saints of our church, the Holy Innocents; and that you are beside God and full of happiness? Would you tell them that you grew to full spiritual maturity and blessedness in the same instant that you left them as a tiny, fragile infant; that you are fulfilled beyond their greatest dreams for you; and that they should rejoice in the knowledge that heaven is altogether astounding, and that you will wait for them to join you there and to enjoy what is now yours?

Would you speak the words of St Paul to them and tell them to keep faith and to look forward because one day they will enjoy with you what you now enjoy, 'what no eye has seen, nor ear heard, nor the heart of man conceived, what God has prepared for those who love him'? (1 Cor 2:9)

Would you tell them to worry only about themselves until they come to where you are; that they are to console and comfort each other with the assurance of how well you are; and that from now on, and throughout their lives, God will allow you a special concern for them by which you will walk their days with them like a guardian angel at their side? Would you tell them that they are only at the start of their married life together; and that God is able to pick up all the pieces and mend them, and all the losses and reshape them?

And would you tell Mum and Dad that the Rachel in the Bible who wept for her lost children and would not be comforted eventually did find comfort, and that she became the mother of other children, Joseph and Benjamin?

And would you tell them that one day you will all meet again as a family; that you will meet in the place which is beyond the reach of death, beyond the reach of every tear, God's place, the place that is our true and eternal home?

St Thérèse, the Little Flower, once said, 'I would like to run through the fields of heaven. I would like to run in its fields where the grass doesn't crumble, where there are beautiful flowers which don't fade, and beautiful children who would be little angels.' *(A Little Book of Thérèse of Lisieux)* St Thérèse is there now, running in the fields of the beautiful flowers that don't fade, running among the beautiful children that are little angels, and one of them is Niamh.

Readings: Wis 4:7-15; 1 Thess 4:13-18; Jn 6:37-40

Seán
(who went into the sea)

We do not want you to be uninformed, brothers and sisters, about those who have died, so that you may not grieve as others do who have no hope. For since we believe that Jesus died and rose again, even so, through Jesus, God will bring with him those who have died. For this we declare to you by the word of the Lord, that we who are alive, who are left until the coming of the Lord, will by no means precede those who have died. For the Lord himself, with a cry of command, with the archangel's call and with the sound of God's trumpet, will descend from heaven, and the dead in Christ will rise first. Then we who are alive, who are left, will be caught up in the clouds together with them to meet the Lord in the air; and so we will be with the Lord forever. Therefore encourage one another with these words.' (1 Thess 4:13-18)

Dear friends:

As all of us so well and so tragically know, Seán and Michael and Luke came down Castle Road and, for whatever reason, could not make the left-hand turn at the bottom but sped across the Prom and into the angry night sea. Michael and Luke survive, and we are grateful; Seán did not, and we are in shock and his lovely family is devastated.

We are here, in overflowing numbers, to try to comfort Seán's family and to try to comfort ourselves. If numbers alone could heal, then the massive outpouring of love and solidarity and support for Seán's family during the past few days, and again today, would have expelled their every sorrow and dried their last tear.

What can I say to Mary and Seán senior, to brothers and sisters Tom, Jimmy, Kathleen and Mary, to Monica, Seán's girlfriend, to the members of the extended family, to Seán's closest friends Michael and Luke, and to so many young, shocked and grieving friends? What can I say to you but tell you to lean on the massive love and support and solidarity of our community which is there for you these sad days, and may you, in the future times, remember it as our testimonial to Seán and as the sign of our great love and concern for you.

Dear young people and friends of Seán: May Seán allow me to say something to you? May he allow me to say that you are not indestructible at the age of 18 or 19, or 15 or 16 for that matter. You are very fragile. All of us are. Life itself is fragile. We have to be careful and even wise if we are to survive into adulthood and middle age and old age. There is no other easy prescription for holding onto life, no magic bullet, no cutting of corners. Nothing is guaranteed in this world; but care and caution are a mighty help.

Now I'm not here to lecture you because when I was your age I, too, felt indestructible, and even eternal. But none of us is. That's a plain fact of life. So please, please live life on its terms, within its rules, with its cautions; otherwise life will be pitiless towards you and the family and the friends who will have to come to this or another church to mourn you.

What did we lose in Seán? Let it be said simply: we lost a superior young man. Why is it so often the good ones who go so soon? We lost a part of the hope and future of our country. We lost what was meant to be a pillar of some community and of some parish down the road. We lost a potential leader, possibly an educator, or a businessman, advisor, politician, public servant, future husband and father, and so charming and loveable a friend. We lost a future that should have been, a dream that could have been, and the promise that might have been realised to the benefit of many.

What can I say to Mary and Seán senior, to Tom, Jimmy, Kathleen and Mary, and to Monica; what can I say? Your loss is beyond my power of description and the hole in your hearts will not be filled by any words I speak. Yet words are all I have.

I could take you, with my words, to the killing fields of the great World Wars where I have been and walk you through

rows upon rows of crosses which mark the graves of hundreds
of thousands of young men, the flower of Europe in their day,
the promise of their nations, the hope of their fathers, the joy of
their mothers, the love of their wives and fiancées and sweet-
hearts. I could read you the war poetry of solemn remembrance,
so beautiful and yet so futile in the face of such destruction and
slaughter and loss and heartbreak. I can only poorly comfort
you now by telling you that all of us here today would wish to
put Seán's name with the names of these young war dead so we
may be allowed to say of him what Laurence Binyon said of
them:

> They shall not grow old, as we that are left grow old:
> Age shall not weary them, nor the years condemn.
> At the going down of the sun and in the morning
> We will remember them.
> *(Poem for the Fallen)*

But remembrance is not enough. Resurrection is so much better.
And we have it because of our faith!

I turn to the word of God to find comfort for you and
promise for Seán. The word of God will not return Seán to you
in this life. It will not return him so he might live to fill in what
are now the blank pages in the book of his life. But the word of
God will point you in hope to the last chapter of his life, and the
last chapter of your own lives. For what has happened so tragically has not changed the last chapter of Seán's life nor of yours. It
is the chapter where Seán and you meet again. The word of God
I'm referring to was our second reading at Mass today, and I will
repeat it, rephrasing it just a little so you may feel the force of its
comfort and of its great promise:

'We want you, beloved, to be clear about those like Seán who
sleep in death, so that you do not give in to grief like people who
have no hope. If we believe that Jesus died and rose from the
dead, God will bring forth with Jesus from the dead all, like
Seán, who have died believing in him. We say to you – as though
the Lord himself were saying it to you – that we who live on,
who survive until the Lord's coming, will in no way have an

advantage over those like Seán who have already died ... At the archangel's call, and with the sound of God's trumpet, those who have died in Christ will rise first. Then we, the living, the survivors, will be caught up with them ... to meet the Lord ... From then on, we shall all be with the Lord forever. Comfort one another with these words.' (1 Thess 4:13-18)

The days ahead will be difficult, especially for you, dear Mary and Seán senior, and Tom, Jimmy, Kathleen, Mary, and Monica, Michael and Luke. They will not lose your sorrow for you nor fully fill the hole in your hearts. But you will live with the grace and the guarantee of God supporting you. You will live in the sure hope of the resurrection, and with the promise that you and lovely Seán will surely meet again.

Readings: Ps 139:1-4, 13-16; Rom 5:5-11; Jn 6:37-40

Owen

(who could not stay longer)

O Lord, you have searched me and you know me.
You know when I sit down and when I rise up;
you discern my thoughts from afar.
You search out my path and my lying down,
and are aquainted with all my ways.
Even before a word is on my tongue,
O Lord, you know it completely ...
For it was you who formed my inward parts;
you knit me together in my mother's womb.
I praise you, for I am fearfully and wonderfully made.
Wonderful are your works;
that I know very well.
My frame was not hidden from you,
when I was being made in secret,
intricately woven in the depths of the earth.
Your eyes beheld my unformed substance.
In your book were written
all the days that were formed for me,
when none of them as yet existed. (Ps 139:1-4, 13-16)

Dear friends:

We gather here at this liturgy in loving support of Paddy and Bridie who have lost dear Owen. It is a time of immense pain and of disorientation for them. What has happened with the death of Owen has not sunk in fully, and they are numbed and almost detached from reality because of it. That is why you and I gather around them, as best we can, straining to support them with our love and our prayers.

When Owen went into the river and out to sea we wished we could believe that it was an accident. Even the horror of someone pushing him in would have been some sort of comfort – an argument over nothing that got out of control, a drunken push not really intended and which would be apologised for next day, a loss of his footing on the wet wintry bank. Anything like that would have eased the shock and lessened the grief of Paddy and Bridie. But we cannot find comfort in such lesser scenarios. They are not what happened.

Owen wanted to go. He left a note. Life was overwhelming him. He was so sorry about this, and he loved Paddy and Bridie, and he asked Sheila and Nano to try to understand.

I'm sure they don't. None of us does. At least not fully. But Owen's family, and especially his dear parents, need some understanding of their loss, and they need some hope for Owen's future beyond this tragedy that threatens to haunt them for the rest of their lives.

You and I wish to help them as best we can. We tell them that we will remember Owen not by how he died but for the quiet and helping young man that we knew him to be. We tell ourselves, and we tell Paddy and Bridie and Sheila and Nano, that a single human act, done in extreme confusion and stress, is something any one of us might do given psychological circumstances we do not even understand. We do not know ourselves so well that we can guarantee what we would, or would not, do under extreme pressure. We recall the wise insight of the words, 'There, but for the grace of God, go I.' And we try to comfort Owen's family and caution ourselves with those words.

We tell Owen's family that all of us here accept that a single unfortunate decision made by Owen in extreme turmoil does not represent, and can never be allowed to represent, the whole life and character of a person, the life and character of the quiet and ever helping Owen.

This is not the place nor the time to ponder the psychology of taking one's own life. But we want to assure Owen's family that suicides, generally, are people at their wit's end. We do our best to accept them as people who, in their stress, have come to believe that 'to live will be more miserable than to die'. (Graham Greene, *The Comedians*) We know enough psychology to realise that suicides lack effective strategies to cope with the awful stress they are under and the unshatterable bind they feel themselves to be in. Perhaps it may help and comfort Owen's family if we say, too, that the experts wish to tell them that it's alright for them, as survivors, to feel abandoned and rejected by Owen as long as they understand that Owen did _not_ reject them at all and did not deliberately wish to abandon them. They should see the truth of that in Owen's last letter in which he expressed his love for them, and told them of the pressure he could bear no longer.

We want the family to know that they are going through the beginning stages of the same grieving process that all bereaved families go through, and that they will eventually recover from this tragedy and from their grief.

We want them to know that we are full of hope in regard to Owen's future with the Lord, so that they may be full of hope too. We quote our friend St Paul who said that God 'is rich in mercy' and so loves us that 'when we were dead through our trespasses' he nonetheless 'made us alive together with Christ'. (Eph 2:4) If God's mercy applies to our deliberate sins, as St Paul says, all the more does God's mercy apply to Owen's unfree and overwhelmed mind.

In faith, we believe that we shall meet Owen again. We shall all meet again in the resurrection and in glory. We shall meet again because our God is not merely a judge but the supreme psychologist. He understands the workings and the intricacies, the strengths and the weaknesses of the human heart and mind in every conceivable circumstance and under every possible condition and grade of stress. The Psalmist says, 'Lord, you discern my thoughts from afar. ... You are acquainted with all my ways ... My frame was not hidden from you, when I was being made in secret ... In your book were written all the days that were formed for me, when none of them as yet existed.' (Ps 139)

May Owen rest with his God in secure peace now, and may Our Lord and his Blessed Mother enfold Paddy and Bridie and Sheila and Nano in their loving arms, and assure them that all will be well with Owen, and that all will be well with them.

DEATH OF A YOUNG MAN
Readings: Wis 4:7-9, 11, 13-14; 2 Tim 2:8-13; Jn 5:24-29

Conor
(whose life was cut short)

But the righteous, though they die early, will be at rest. For old age is not honoured for length of time, or measured by number of years; but understanding is grey hair for anyone, and a blameless life is ripe old age ... They were caught up so that evil might not change their understanding or guile deceive their souls ... Being perfected in a short time, they fulfilled long years; for their souls were pleasing to the Lord, therefore he took them quickly from the midst of wickedness. (Wis 4:7-9, 11, 13-14)

Dear friends:

Conor was not long out of university and not long in his software development job, as we all know. His studies were behind him, his life was before him, and the possibilities of the world were at his feet. He was a GAA man through and through like his father before him. He didn't drink, he didn't smoke, he drove carefully, and there was every reason why he should look forward to a long life. He was immensely popular, he had no enemies, but he had a heart attack on the 10th green, and he's dead. And Molly and Gabe are heartbroken over the loss of their only child.

And what are we to say to them when we hardly know what to say to ourselves in the shock of this tragedy?

There are two ways to stand and anguish before tragedy. We can either curse it with the hopelessness of the world or accept it with the help of the word of God.

In the world's view Conor's early death is pure loss. It cannot be viewed in any other light. In the world's utilitarian view his death is meaningless, his life futile. It lasted only as long as the preparation part of it. He was conceived, carried in the womb, born, reared, trained and fretted over by his parents. He consumed a share of the nation's food and medical resources, was educated for almost twenty-two years, and to what purpose? The state invested some of its money in him and society invested its hope of the future in him, and their investments have yielded nothing.

And the manner of his death? – to die while exercising, to die on the 10th green of a golf course, to die where young men are supposed to rejoice: there is contradiction and tragedy here. Conor's life is kin to all the young lives of history that we mourn over, the lives snuffed out too soon, the lives that were no more than prefaces. In this view, there is no future other than the early grave for the likes of Conor, and no solace for Molly and Gabe that makes sense. Death is the end. Death is annihilation. Death came too soon.

The philosopher, Socrates, thought about all of this and spoke of another possibility. 'Death,' he said, 'is either annihilation ... or a change: a migration of the soul from this place to another.' (in Plato, *Apology*) Socrates thought that death does not have to be the world's view of it, the view of waste and futility, the view of early annihilation. The first reading of our Mass, from the Book of Wisdom, talks to us instead about Socrates' second view, the view of change. In this view, Conor's soul has not been annihilated: it has gone from this place to God's place.

Such a view, of course, requires religious faith. It requires faith at any time and especially today. More and more people today measure the life of a young person by its length and not by its quality, and certainly not by its spiritual quality. On the other hand, the Book of Wisdom, a training manual for Jewish young men, recognises the misfortune of a life cut short but puts it in the wider perspective of a life well-lived. Shortness of years is not of the essence of life at all: the moral quality of its years is.

We heard some of Wisdom's hopeful statements in the first reading. The 'righteous man,' says the Book of Wisdom, even though he die young, has achieved the primary purpose of life and is 'at rest' now in God. The primary purpose of life is 'righteousness' and the attainment of heaven. 'Old age,' says the Book of Wisdom, is not 'length of years' but 'understanding,' i.e. spiritual wisdom. 'Old age' is spiritual wisdom, and 'ripe old age,' says the Book of Wisdom, is 'a blameless life'.

Conor was of a wise and blameless life as all of us know from his practise of the faith and from the moral quality of his life, from his sensitivity to others' needs and his kindly disposition. In this sense, he already attained the goal of old age which is the blameless life. The Book of Wisdom says of Conor, 'Being perfected in a short time, he fulfilled long years. His soul was pleasing to the Lord, therefore he took him quickly.' Seen in the light of the word of God, Conor's life was not futile but fulfilled.

I know, dear Molly and Gabe, that while these scriptures comfort you with the assurance that Conor attained the primary purpose of his life and is at rest in God, you are still left with an empty chair at home and a huge emptiness in your hearts. The Book of Wisdom will not fill those spaces. But the support of those who love you and the grace of God will help you through all the stages of your loss and mourning.

The word of God tells you that you will meet Conor again. Death ends nothing for him as a Christian. For Christ's resurrection has destroyed the hold of death over us. You and Conor will meet again in the resurrection. You will meet again beyond this mis-calibrated world and beyond this broken life with its too few years and too many tears. Jesus said, 'Truly, truly, I say to you, he who hears my word and believes him who sent me, has eternal life; he does not come to judgement, but has passed from death to life.' (Jn 5:24)

May I speak this prayer of offering in your names, dear Molly and Gabe, because I know the depth of your trust in the Sacred Heart?:

Lord, we give our loved one back to you,
and just as you first gave him to us
and did not lose him in the giving,
so we have not lost him
in returning him to you.
For life is eternal,

love is immortal,
death is only an horizon,
and an horizon is nothing
but the limit of our earthly sight.
We hold him close within our hearts,
and there he shall remain,
to walk with us throughout our lives
until we meet again.
(*Jubilee Prayer Book*, Salthill Parish)

Readings: *Wis 4:7-15; Rom 8:14-18; Jn 11:17-27*

Cáit

(whose exit so moves us)

When Jesus arrived, he found that Lazarus had already been in the tomb four days. Now Bethany was near Jerusalem, some two miles away, and many of the Jews had come to Martha and Mary to console them about their brother. When Martha heard that Jesus was coming, she went and met him, while Mary stayed at home. Martha said to Jesus, 'Lord, if you had been here my brother would not have died. But even now I know that God will give you whatever you ask of him.' Jesus said to her, 'Your brother will rise again.' Martha said to him, 'I know that he will rise again in the resurrection on the last day.' Jesus said to her, 'I am the resurrection and the life. Those who believe in me, even though they die, will live, and everyone who lives and believes in me will never die. Do you believe this?' She said to him, 'Yes, Lord, I believe that you are the Messiah, the Son of God, the one coming into the world.' (Jn 11:23-27)

Dear friends:

These days people live much longer than their ancestors. To die, like Cáit, at twenty-seven is to die in the springtime of life. It is to die in the season which contradicts death, when nature everywhere is signalling re-birth after winter.

Spring! 'The snows have fled,' wrote Horace in the *Odes*, 'already the grass is returning to the fields and the leaves to the trees.' For Gerard Manley Hopkins,

Nothing is so beautiful as spring –
When weeds, in wheels, shoot long and lovely and lush;
Thrush's eggs look like low heavens, and thrush
Through the echoing timber does so rinse and ring
The ear, it strikes like lightnings to hear him sing ...
(*Spring*)

Of the new riot of colour and life and lushness, Rainer Maria

Rilke wrote beautifully, 'Spring has returned. The earth is like a child that knows poems.' *(Sonnets to Orpheus)* But here are you and I burying Cáit in the springtime of her lovely life and talent!

Cáit was a joy among us. She had that beautiful face and vivacious spirit that drew you to her company and made you feel good to be alive on any day or in any season of the year. She had that natural charm that drew her, in turn, into the companionship of every age and social bracket from the elderly to little children. She was one of those infrequent but truly blessed persons for whom human outreach is effortless and communication a natural ingredient of their personality. People instinctively wanted Cáit's company – and wanted her to join every organisation in the parish, and far beyond its boundaries.

She joined many of them. She was in civil defence, the ICA, meals-on-wheels, the golf club, and the *Journal* editorial committee. She was active with one of the prayer groups, a reader here in church, a member of the choir, and a eucharistic minister to the sick. She helped to organise tours to Europe's Marian shrines, and once a month she went to Knock for her turn as a handmaid there.

Her special love was acting. Even as an amateur, she shone on the stage. We all saw her in the town hall or in the regional and national amateur drama festivals and enjoyed and applauded her great gift.

John B., as you well know, thought her *Sive* was as good as it gets, and Richard Harris one time saw her future on the boards – should she ever turn professional – as the sure unfolding of a national artistic treasure.

All this personal, social and spiritual richness of Cáit's life makes it all the more difficult for us to let go of her. But we let go of her in faith, knowing full well where she is going and not wishing to refuse God the pleasure of her company which we ourselves have so enjoyed. She was his gift and grace on loan to us – we must never forget that – and she was an outstanding gift and grace. Can we even say we are the poorer for her passing from us when her presence was so potent and so simply beautiful and gracious that its remembrance will long remain as a living thing among us? Few souls have that kind of effect on those among whom they live for however long or short a span. But Cáit did.

We will not waste time, then, mulling over the ifs and buts of her fatal car crash. We will not waste time wishing in vain against the passing of her life from us and God taking her back to himself. For we have our exits and our entrances in this world, as Shakespeare noted in *As You Like It*, and Cáit has made her final exit. We will remember, instead, the beauty and the love and the charm and the joy and the talent that she was among us. Cáit and her grace and gifts will long linger in our hearts:

I feel no anger at your death,
Flailing and floundering though I am
In loss;
More
An upsurge of gratitude
For the way you blessed us:

We have known the bounty of Autumn
And settle into Winter
With harvest of rich apples.

(Pádraig J. Daly, 'Remembering Paddy', *The Last Dreamers*)

To Cáit's Mum and Dad, we offer our deepest sympathy. We offer them the love of this congregation that gathers around them now and the strength they receive from the grace of this Mass. May I say to Bridget and Al, and to Cáit, and to all of you, and to myself: We will all meet again in the resurrection because of the loving plan and pure goodness of our God. Our lives are intertwined and nothing is, in fact, really ended.

For we hear these promising words in the gospel reading of our Mass, and we take them to our hearts full of hope: 'Jesus said to her, "Your brother will rise again." Martha said to him, "I know that he will rise again in the resurrection on the last day." Jesus said to her, "I am the resurrection and the life. Those who believe in me, even though they die, will live, and everyone who lives and believes in me will never die. Do you believe this?" She said to him, "Yes, Lord, I believe that you are the Messiah, the Son of God, the one coming into the world".' (Jn 11:23-27)

Readings: Is 25:6-9; Phil 3:20-21; Jn 14:1-6

Jim
(who called us many names)

Jesus said, 'Do not let your hearts be troubled. Believe in God, believe also in me. In my Father's house are many dwelling places. If it were not so, would I have told you that I go to prepare a place for you? And if I go and prepare a place for you, I will come again and will take you to myself, so that where I am, there you may be also.' (Jn 14:1-4)

Dear friends:

We gather here at this eucharist to send Jim on his final journey. May I begin by thanking you, the parishioners, for your solidarity with Jim at this time. I had asked about a dozen of you to be sure to show up – and here we have at least a hundred!

May I thank the Gardaí, too, and the university hospital staff, and the funeral directors for their *gratis* service, and the county for what an older generation called 'the narrow bed' in the New Cemetery.

In one sense, you and I knew Jim well. In another sense, we didn't know him at all. We knew him for the wrong reasons. He pestered the priests and he pestered you. He 'disturbed the peace' of the pews on more occasions than we care to count, and sometimes in the middle of Mass it became extremely distracting. I thank you for your tolerance of the years.

Jim even lay down to block your steps and mine when we refused him the five pounds or the ten Euro that we knew would only go on drink, thereby increasing his troubles and unsettling our consciences. By way of revenge, he would park himself on the presbytery porch by day and by night until the children grew afraid or parish business suffered and the only solution was to call the Guards. They were always helpful to us, and understanding of Jim even to a fault. I believe that they are about the only people on the westside that Jim didn't have it in for!

Jim lived in a world of his own inside his head as much as any non-institutionalised person I've known on this side of the Atlantic or the other. Therefore, I sometimes wondered if you and I and the parish had any positive influence on him at all. We didn't seem to have, because every encounter with Jim was sure to turn sour to the exasperation of both him and ourselves. He called us many names, and none too pleasant!

And yet he kept coming back to us like a bad penny – or was it a homing pigeon? Maybe he kept coming back to fight with us because he knew we wouldn't really hurt him, or because in some way he had made us his substitute family. He could fight and let off steam among us, and that was a lot safer than fighting and letting off steam in some tough pub or back alleyway of the city. God works in mysterious ways, scripture tells us, and maybe in that way or in some such manner we were a party to how God worked mysteriously with Jim for his survival on the streets and for his eternal salvation.

It would be nice to think that Jim found support – and grace – of some kind while he was among us, and that God kept pushing him back into our path for that reason. William Bausch tells a story that may or may not fit the bill with regard to Jim and ourselves. I sincerely hope it does. It is a story about sequoia trees. Sequoias are giant trees. In California, where I lived much of my life, we also called them redwoods. They grow as tall as three hundred feet and can have a trunk diameter of thirty feet! In fact, I've driven through a forest of them in Northern California, some believed to be as old as 3500 years.

This, then, is Bausch's story and I would like to imagine that we and Jim are to be found in it:

While on a tour of California's giant sequoia trees, the guide pointed out that the sequoia tree has roots just barely below the surface. Someone exclaimed, 'That's impossible! I'm a country boy, and I know that if the roots don't grow deep into the earth, strong winds will blow the trees over.' The guide replied, 'Not sequoia trees. They grow only in groves and their roots intertwine under the surface of the earth. So, when the strong winds come, they hold each other up.' (A World Of Stories)

May it be that in our own small way we helped to hold Jim up in the storms of the last years of his life. He had a troubled life, God rest him. He bothered others, and was bothered by them. The trouble and the bother are over now, and we send him back to God through this funeral liturgy. We are at peace about him. And he is at peace. We trust in the Lord's word for him. We visualise Jesus saying to him even now, 'Do not let your heart be troubled, Jim. ... In my Father's house are many dwelling places. If it were not so, would I have told you that I go to prepare a place for you? And if I go and prepare a place for you, I will come again and will take you to myself, so that where I am, there you may be also.'